**In t**[he Names of]

Ibis Headed Thoth & Starry Crowned Isis,
of Hard Visaged Athena & Brightly Winged Hermes,
of the Clever Legba & the Wise Erzulie Freda,
of Melodious Sarasvati & the Graceful Dancing Ganesh,
and of All Other Divinities of Wisdom, Art, & Science;

## A Spell

is Hereby Placed upon All who Read these Words!

## If

You should Steal this Book
or Borrow it and Return it Not
to its Rightful Owner,

## Who is:

_____

## Or If

You should Use this Book for any Rite or Spell
that would Injure or Enslave any Innocent Person
or Cause Harm to Our Holy Mother Earth,

## Then Shall

All your Tools and Weapons Turn against you,
All Beauty and Joy Depart from your Life,
and All your Cunning Avail you Naught
Save Sorrow and Despair,
Till you have Made Full Restitution
for your Crime.

*Caveant Malefactores!*

Isaac Bonewits, 2005

# BONEWITS'S
## ESSENTIAL GUIDE
## TO WITCHCRAFT
## AND WICCA

## ISAAC BONEWITS

With a Preface and an Appendix
by Ashleen O'Gaea

And an Appendix by Jenny Gibbons

CITADEL PRESS
Kensington Publishing Corp.
www.kensingtonbooks.com

CITADEL PRESS BOOKS are published by

Kensington Publishing Corp.
850 Third Avenue
New York, NY 10022

Portions of this work were originally published in ebook format by PocketPCpress
as *Witchcraft: A Concise History* in 2001
and in trade paperback format by Virtual Publishing Group, Inc. & Earth Religions Press
as *Witchcraft: A Concise Guide* in 2001.
Portions previously published in html format
on the author's website: www.neopagan.net.
"Reconciling with the Moon" © 2001 by Ashleen O'Gaea
first published in *Circle Magazine*, Summer 2001.
"Recent Developments in the Study of the Great European Witch Hunt"
© 1998 by Jenny Gibbons
first published in *Pomegranate #5*.

Cover design inspired by Robin Wood's flowering pentacle.

All Kensington titles, imprints, and distributed lines are available at special quantity
discounts for bulk purchases for sales promotions, premiums, fund-raising, educational, or
institutional use. Special book excerpts or customized printings can also be created to fit
specific needs. For details, write or phone the office of the Kensington special sales
manager: Kensington Publishing Corp., 850 Third Avenue, New York, NY 10022, attn:
Special Sales Department; phone 1-800-221-2647.

CITADEL PRESS and the Citadel logo are Reg. U.S. Pat. & TM Off.

First printing: February 2006

10  9  8  7  6  5  4  3  2  1

Printed in the United States of America

Library of Congress Control Number: 2005934012

ISBN 0-8065-2711-0

This book is dedicated to:

All My Priestesses
(soon to be a major motion picture)
who have revealed more faces of the Goddess
than mythographers ever know—
not just Maiden, Mother, or Crone
but also Trickster, Lover, Bard, and Editor.

and to:
Elspeth, Nybor, and Mara
(they know why)

*"She changes everything She touches and
everything She touches changes."*

# Contents

## Part Four: Wiccan Beliefs and Rituals

## Appendices: Wiccan Resources and References

# Foreword

## by Ashleen O'Gaea

hich witch is which? That was (at least comparatively) an easy question to answer back in the 1960s when Rosemary and Ray Buckland brought Wicca to the United States. There were, then, a few self-styled "witches-with-a-small-w," and there were Gardnerians (followers of the religion started by Gerald Gardner and his friends in the 1940s, see chapter 8) and Gardnerian-trained entrepreneurs. But after fifty years of sometimes explosive growth in the United States and around the world, it's hard to tell the players even with a scorecard. *Bonewits's Essential Guide to Witchcraft and Wicca* is better than a scorecard.

Now, any Neopagan author *could* do at least most of the same research Bonewits has done over the years, but not many Wiccan authors have *bothered*. There's been a trend in the last decade toward a development of new Traditions (denominations) rather than to look deeply into the origins of Neopaganism or delve into the magical and ethical principles underlying Wiccan practice.

That's been exciting, and certainly worthwhile—but now that Wicca is reasonably well known and still growing, it's more important than ever that we Witches get a handle on our history and a precise command of our vocabulary. If we don't, we risk not just stalling Wicca's growth, but setting it back.

Isaac Bonewits has been doing reality checks for Wicca for a number of years now. Initiated into "one of the most distinguished (and prolific) of all the Gardnerian 'family lines' in America," he knows

Wicca from the inside out, and in this work he shares the definitions and distinctions he's developed from his intimate experience and original research. When you're talking about Neopagan Witchcraft, Bonewits is an author, advisor, and scholar you want—no, let me be stronger—he's someone you *need* on your side.

When we use the word "witch," what do we mean? How do we distinguish the Traditions of Wicca? How old is this religion, anyway? These are questions that the Neopagan community has debated for half a century, and they come up again for every generation of Wiccans. There are other books that discuss them, but none so concise as this one, and consequently, none so useful.

For forty years or more, Witches have worked to earn mainstream religions' and other institutions' acknowledgment of Wicca as a "real" religion, worthy of respect. Thanks to this effort—always hard and sometimes perilous—Wicca is recognized now, and it's better understood and accepted every day. But every time someone speaks from ignorance, or speaks imprecisely about Wicca—even if the error's not noticed immediately—it sets that work back and disrespects our forebears and colleagues. With this *Essential Guide* in hand, all of us can uphold Wicca's reputation accurately.

Bonewits makes it easy to understand Wicca's history and structure meaningfully. Beyond that, he offers one of the best bibliographies I've seen—his reading list alone makes this book indispensable on any serious priest's or priestess's bookshelf. But there's something else that makes this book special, and that's how reader-friendly it is. It's scholarly enough to be worthwhile reading, but it's far from dry or boring, and short enough to take along wherever you go. The chapters and appendices are clearly titled, and that makes this book easy to use as a reference: you don't have to read the whole book every time you're looking for a particular fascinating detail or discussion.

From the history of "our words," to the development and distinction of Wiccan Traditions, to the order of our services, to recommended books and online resources, Bonewits takes us on a tour of Wicca, blending an initiate's point of view with a sociological perspective. Here is the context and commentary we all need to discuss Wicca intelligently among ourselves, with other Neopagans, and with non-Pagans.

As for the self-styled "witches-with-a-small-w" that came out of their broom closets when Wicca made its appearance in the United States? Who better than the man who coined the terms by which we know them now—"Fam-Trads" and "Imm-Trads"—to talk about their place in the modern Craft community?

Call *Bonewits's Essential Guide to Witchcraft and Wicca* a Wiccan *Cliff's Notes* if you will. Bonewits's years of research are summarized here as he guides readers step by step through the histories and diverse origins of the various Wiccan Traditions. In his appendices, he presents equally well-researched and useful material that transforms background information into commonsense and practical applications. This book is an argument-settler, and one you'll want to carry and quote for years to come.

ASHLEEN O'GAEA is the author of *The Family Wicca Book* as well as *Raising Witches: Teaching the Pagan Faith to Children*.

# Preface

f you had gone to any online bookseller's Web site in late 2005 and done a search for books with "witch" or "Wicca" in their titles, you would have received over 5,000 listings. So why should I add another to the pile, and why should you consider adding this one to your library? Because Sturgeon's law* ("90 percent of everything is crud") holds as true for magical and religious books as it does for science fiction—and some would say 90 percent is being overly generous! The last twenty years have seen an explosion of books about ancient and modern witchcraft by both the friends and enemies of whatever the authors thought witchcraft was. A wide variety of definitions have been offered by these books' authors for the words "witch," "witchcraft," and "Wicca," and often the authors don't clarify how their definitions match or differ from those of other writers. This can leave the would-be student of the topic greatly confused.

More important, during those twenty years a number of new works of scholarship on the topic of witchcraft have been published (and some older ones have been brought to my attention), ones that have completely overturned much of what we thought we knew about ancient and modern witchcraft. Authors such as Robin Briggs (*Witches and Neighbors*), Stuart Clark (*Thinking with Demons*), and Ronald Hutton (*Triumph of the Moon*) have dramatically altered our

*Theodore Sturgeon, originally writing about the quality of writing in science-fiction fanzines.

knowledge of medieval, Renaissance, and revivalist witches. Many of my suspicions about the claims of modern Wiccans concerning our supposed predecessors have turned out to have been insufficiently skeptical and overly generous*—everything we knew *was* wrong, based (sometimes deliberately) on obsolete scholarship and sloppy thinking. This has forced me to dramatically rewrite some sections of this work in the process of updating it for what amounts to a fourth edition.

So at the risk of having this appear at first glance to be just another "Wicca 101" book, I decided to expand this text to become *Bonewits's Essential Guide to Witchcraft and Wicca*—a touchstone text that can be used to organize and direct a reader's studies in the field for several years. When combined with the books and resources mentioned in the footnotes and the appendices, the information in these pages will guide the beginner safely into becoming an experienced witch and/or Wiccan, while giving some of his or her elders in the Craft new data and tips to improve both their theory and their practice—making it a "Wicca 301" book as well.

What readers won't find is (a) spells to cast or (b) arguments that one particular way of witchcraft or Wicca is the best one for all people. There are plenty of books in the market that are full of spells you can do, and as a Neopagan pluralist, I am more than willing to let there be as many varieties of witchcraft as people want there to be (although I will express my opinions about certain varieties of Wicca being dysfunctional, abusive, or irrational).

I apologize for some of the back-and-forth historical jumps in the first several chapters of this work. I decided that a thematic approach based on discussing various definitions (and their related theories) of witchcraft would be less confusing to the average student than a strictly chronological approach. Fortunately, there are many chronologically organized history books mentioned in the footnotes and bibliography, which should be of value to those desiring a decade-by-decade picture.

---

*I may have to retest for my curmudgeon's license.

## My Biases

Most authors never tell their readers what their personal religious, scholarly, philosophical, or political biases are, but I think it's something readers should know. My religious background as a Neopagan writer, teacher, and priest is rooted in my studies of Druidism, Wicca/Witchcraft, and Asatru (or Norse Paganism), as well as my experiences in Voodoo and Santeria. My opinions have been heavily influenced by folkloric and anthropological studies in world religions, modern occult and parapsychological research, and my participation in the evolution of the American Neopagan movement.* Unlike many other Pagan authors, I've been an opponent of imperial neo-garmentism† from the beginning of my career, so I have no problem calling things as I see them. I feel no obligation to justify Paganism or my opinions about it in terms that will please members of hostile belief systems. In fact, I'm afraid that I'll express a lot of opinions in this work that might offend or annoy those belonging to conservative mainstream religious or otherwise dogmatic faiths. I understand that they want to continue to dominate the universe of religious discourse in the Western world, but thanks to mass communications technology, it is now impossible for them to force everyone on the planet to use their monotheistic, scientistic,‡ or dualistic definitions and values when talking about spiritual matters.

For those wondering about my Wiccan biases, I can say that I practiced a bit of nonreligious witchcraft (i.e., folk magic) before I heard of Wicca, and have since undergone initiations into and the

---

*See Margot Adler's *Drawing Down the Moon* and Rosemary Guiley's entry on me in her *Encyclopedia of Witches and Witchcraft* for details.

†It might be "treason" to mention that the emperor has no clothes, but somebody's got to say it.

‡Scientism is the worship of modern science and the belief that all nonmaterial entities (beings or things) are nonexistent and that therefore all other religions are merely superstitions. It's very much like Christian dualism, only "true" and "false" have been flipped from their Christian attributions to spirit and matter, respectively, to the opposite positions.

practice of both orthodox conservative and liberal heterodox varieties of Wicca, so I believe that I can discuss the different paths with a reasonable amount of neutrality, having seen the strengths and weaknesses of each approach.

My scholarly and philosophical biases are those of an amateur scholar who respects the basic principles of Western science and scholarship and the ideals of the Enlightenment, while recognizing their dualistic and scientistic biases and limitations. Painful as it may sometimes be, when new information comes into the world of academia from legitimate scholarship, I can and will change my mind and what I teach to match the new data. Fortunately, as Neopagans we are not bound to the fossilized words of ancient scriptures or to the writings of old dead men.* We are free to adapt and evolve our religions to match what we learn from science and scholarship.

As for my political biases, I'm a capital "L" Liberal and a cardcarrying member of both the American Civil Liberties Union and the Green Party. So now the reader can filter what I have to say through these particular screens, based on her or his own biases!

## Unusual Word Usages in This Book†

I try to avoid offending anyone accidentally and I dislike language customs that oversimplify matters that are complex or that conceal hidden or unverified assumptions. So I've gotten in the habit over the years of using terms such as "and/or" and "his/her." These read somewhat clumsily to most current English speakers, as do various nonsexist terms such as "chairperson" or "clergyperson," yet these usages are actually more precise than the older ones, since they don't carry the excess baggage of hidden implications (to many people, a word like "clergyman," for example, implies that only men can be clergy).

Those slash marks, as well as parentheses, come in quite handy

---

*I may be old, but "I'm not dead yet!"

†Those familiar with my opinions on this topic from my other books are free to skip this section.

when discussing ambiguous topics (a frequent need in books that deal with magic and religion). For example, "god/dess" means a deity who can be thought of in terms of either or both genders, "priest/ess" can mean a priest and/or a priestess, depending on the situation, and so on. Once you've seen a few of these, the rest will be easy to figure out from their context.

Perhaps more annoying to English-language purists is my occasional use of "they," "them," and "their" when discussing individuals of deliberately unspecified gender. Sometimes we also need the plural/singular distinction kept vague, and parentheses work well with ambiguous pronouns for this, as in the sentence "You should practice with your working partner(s), otherwise they may not understand what they are supposed to do." Such usages are now quite common in idiomatic American English precisely because the common people (if not the grammarians) have learned that ambiguous terms are often useful. The context should make clear which of several meanings are appropriate for the reader to understand.

As for capitalization quirks, the terms "Pagan," "Paleopagan," "Mesopagan," and "Neopagan" will be capitalized just as the names of other religions and their members are. Similarly, when the word "witch" refers to someone who belongs to a religious form of Witchcraft, or when I am referring to a specific category of Witchcraft, it will be capitalized.

Most of the time, I use italic text the first time I define a term and quote marks when referring to the word as a word later. I also use italics for foreign words, emphasis, the names of books and periodicals, and so on.

Since this book was written simultaneously with several others, I've had to divide related materials between them. These books and earlier ones will therefore be frequently referenced in each other's pages, though I try to make each work capable of standing on its own.

# Acknowledgments

his book is the product of many years of reading scholarly works, some of them well respected by their colleagues, some heretical (then or now), and a few genuinely ground-breaking ones here and there. Just as important in many ways, however, have been the words and actions of those brave (or foolhardy) women and men who have founded, invented, stolen, modified, mutated, and otherwise perpetuated the many old and new systems of magic and religion that I have been informed for forty years by them were what "Witchcraft" was really all about.

At the risk of offending someone whose name I am sure to forget, I would like to specifically mention and thank the following as having helped along the way—whether they meant to or not—with knowledge, wisdom, and wit:

Margot Adler, Victor Anderson, Gavin Bone, Robin Briggs, Skip Clark, Stuart Clark, Scott Cunningham, Aliester Crowley, Georges Dumézil, Mircea Eliade, Janet Farrar, Stuart Farrar, Donald Frew, Gavin Frost, Gerald Gardner, Ronald Hutton, Richard James, Tamara James, Aiden Kelly, Frederick Lamond, Sybil Leek, Patricia Monaghan, Jeffrey Burton Russell, Starhawk, Doreen Valiente, and Carl Weschke. Other authors whose works influenced this book are mentioned in appendix 5 (and parenthetical comments to "see So-and-So" refer to books there).

The following are some of those who have shown me the many

ways that the Goddess can manifest inside a Wiccan circle: Arlynde de Laughlin, Sally Eaton, Rusty Elliott, Yvonne Frost, Magenta Griffiths, Elspeth of Haven, Phaedra Heyman, Anodea Judith, Alta Kelly, Deborah Lipp, Selene Vega, and Gaia Wildwood. My knowledge of Wiccan priestcraft would be considerably poorer without their priestess-craft.

I would also like to thank again Ashleen O'Gaea for her gracious foreword, as well as thank her for permission to include her essay "Reconciling with the Moon." Thanks are also due to Jenny Gibbons, who has allowed me to include her very important essay "Recent Developments in the Study of the Great European Witch Hunt." Bob Shuman, my first editor at Citadel Press, asked me a number of insightful and interesting questions, which enabled me to make this edition more reader-friendly and useful to the first-time student.

# Bonewits's Essential Guide to Witchcraft and Wicca

# Introduction

Let us sing some verses for our predecessors bold,
Who revived the worship of the Gods of old.
Let us raise our glasses now, of cider, wine or beer:
If it hadn't been for them back then, we'd none of us
    be here!

*Dreamers and scholars, poets and rakes,*
*Some of them real and some of them fakes;*
*Still we love our moms and dads—*
*They're the ones who started all of our new Pagan trads.* *

## The Myth of Wicca

nce upon a time, say 10,000 years ago, there was a Universal Goddess Cult all over ancient Europe and the Middle East. This was the central religion of a peaceful, neolithic matriarchy. Then those mean, nasty, patriarchal barbarians came along, raping, looting, and pillaging everywhere they went. They destroyed the matriarchy and enslaved the women, replacing the Universal Goddess Cult with new religions in which male deities were supreme. Nonetheless, some goddesses were kept as wives, daughters, or lovers of the male gods, and these goddesses had their priestesses who served them in temples everywhere.

Then the even meaner, nastier, and more patriarchal Christians came along, crushing the Old Religion (which had been the same everywhere) and slaughtering its clergy. The survivors went into hiding

---

*"Dreamers and Scholars," © 1990, 1999 by Isaac Bonewits, sung more or less to the tune of "Turkey in the Straw."

1

and kept the Old Religion alive during all the centuries of Christian tyranny, worshipping the Triple Goddess as Mother, Maiden, and Crone and the Horned God as a two-aspected solar and hunting-vegetation deity. The secret priests and priestesses were the witches, who were beloved healers, midwives, and spell-casters for the peasants (and a select few of the nobility).

The Church of Rome knew about the Old Religion, considered it a threat, and hated and feared the innocent witches, who never, ever hurt anyone except bad guys who deserved it. So the Inquisition was started to hunt down and torture the witches, forcing them to confess to being worshippers of the Christians' Devil god, then burning nine million women from Russia and Greece, to Sweden, Scotland, and New England.

But they failed in their efforts to completely wipe out the faith and now it has revived from many hidden families of witches who kept the Old Religion alive as part of their secret family traditions, which they will share with you if you buy their books.

And anyone who doesn't believe all of this is a poopyhead who hates the Goddess!

## Images of Witchcraft

An old crone shuffles out of her hovel at the edge of the village, going into the garden behind her home. Slowly and painfully she cuts a few sprigs of moonwort and adderstongue, pulls a few leaves of devilsnose and foxglove, then pulls up a couple of carrots and a turnip. Returning to the dark interior of her home, she throws the herbs into a small cauldron of boiling water in her hearth and the vegetables into the larger one in which she is cooking her dinner. She mumbles a few odd words over the two cauldrons as she stirs them, then dredges up the herbs and wraps them in a rag. Turning to her visitor, she says, "Put this on your leg and tie it into place. Leave it there overnight, then come back in the morning—with another chicken!" Her visitor hands over the plucked chicken he had been holding, receives the poultice, says his thanks, and swiftly departs. Already forgetting him, she turns to the task of cleaning and cooking his payment, grateful for the rare bit of meat.

It's a full moon and deep in the forest evil monsters (who look just like people, only really ugly or really good looking) are stealthily making their way through the night. Those in the air are riding brooms or pitchforks, while those on the ground are walking, using foul-smelling candles made from human fat to guide their way. By ones and by twos, they enter a small moonlit clearing, where they are greeted by a man dressed like the Devil—or perhaps it's the Devil himself—who forces them to kiss him under his tail as a way of showing their allegiance. When all have arrived, a blasphemous ritual is performed, the people desecrating holy objects with various bodily fluids, murdering a few babies, then cooking and eating the flesh of the poor victims. During the unholy meal, the Devil teaches those assembled how to curse their neighbors and cast love spells on the unwary. After a few hours of wild dancing, drinking, and carousing, the inhuman fiends fall on each other in a frenzy of bestial lust, ignoring all decent bounds of family or marriage. The orgy continues until a distant cockcrow warns them to flee homeward before their unsuspecting friends and family can notice that they aren't at home in their beds.

Great-grandpa knew all about horses and how to get them to do what you wanted by whispering certain words in their ears. He was also a 32nd-degree Freemason and a Rosicrucian, who used to attend Spiritualist séances. He taught what he learned to his kids and they to theirs. Now your mom says it's your turn to learn how to use a Ouija board or make the vegetable garden grow better.

It's a full moon in a different century, and half a dozen people are meeting in a suburban living room. One woman picks up a sword from a small altar in the middle, then walks around the room tracing a circle on the carpet. The people in the circle invoke elemental spirits in the four directions, then ask the Goddess to possess the woman, so She can speak through Her priestess. This happens, and the Goddess gives the assembled people advice and teaching on healing spells and job magic. Then the group does a couple of spells under Her direction, sending their energies out into the world to work their will. After the ceremony, everyone hangs out and socializes until it's time to go home and relieve their babysitters.

So are some, all, or none of these people "real witches"? People doing (or believed to be doing) all these activities have been called witches at one time or another over the last fifteen centuries or so. In the pages that follow, we will meet these various kinds of witches and see what we can find out about them. Over the course of this book we will consider all the arguments for and against the Myth of Wicca and the various images of witchcraft. First, however, I should define some important terms for those who might not be familiar with them.


## Paleo-, Meso-, and Neopaganism*

The history of the term *Pagan* is long and complex, and during most of it the word was used as an insult. Today, there are many people who proudly call *ourselves* Pagan, and we use the word differently from the ways that most mainstream Westerners do. To us, "Pagan" is a general term for religions that are polytheistic (have multiple deities) and/or pan(en)theistic (believing that the divine is everywhere and/or is in everything), and usually focused on nature, whether those faiths are old or new, as well as their members.

That, however, tends to be too broad a definition for many uses, so subcategories have been named:

*Paleopaganism* refers to the original tribal faiths of Europe, Africa, Asia, the Americas, Oceania, and Australia, when they were (or in some cases, still are) practiced as intact belief systems. Of the so-called Great Religions of the World, Classic Hinduism (before the influx of Islam into India), Taoism (before the arrival of Buddhism), and Shinto (ditto) fall under this category.

---

*This discussion is taken from my *Rites of Worship: A Neopagan Approach*.

*Mesopaganism* is the word used for those religions founded as attempts to re-create, revive, or continue what their founders *thought of* as the "traditional" Paleopagan ways of their ancestors (or predecessors), but that were heavily influenced (accidentally, deliberately, or involuntarily) by the monotheistic and dualistic worldviews of Judaism, Christianity, and/or Islam (or nontheistic Buddhism). Examples of Mesopagan belief systems would include Freemasonry, Rosicrucianism, Spiritualism, and Druidism as practiced by the Masonic-influenced fraternal movements in Europe and the Celtic Isles, the many African Diasporic faiths (such as Voudoun, Santeria, or Macumba), Sikhism, and most of modern Hinduism, all of which have been influenced by Islam and/or Christianity. Hinduism has also been influenced by Buddhism, as have Taoism, Shinto, and the Tibetan Bon religion. Many liberal religious movements, such as Christian Science, New Thought, Unity, and so on can be thought of as Mesopagan, though their founders and some current members might be horrified to do so. And as we shall see, most of Europe's Christians through much of its history were unconscious Mesopagans.

*Neopaganism* refers to those religions created since 1960 or so (though many of them had literary roots going back to the mid-1800s) that have attempted to blend what their founders perceived as the best aspects of different types of Paleopaganism with modern "Aquarian Age" ideals, while consciously striving to eliminate as much as possible of the traditional Western monotheism and dualism.

The Roman Church used the term "neopaganism" to criticize Renaissance artists who enjoyed depicting ancient Greek and Roman deities, while some modern historians have used it to describe the perverted Germanic Mesopaganism invented by the Nazis. The Renaissance artists may have been close in lifestyles and attitudes to modern Neopagans, however, neither of these usages has anything to do with modern Neopaganism.

These terms do not delineate clear-cut categories. Historically, there were often periods, whether of decades or centuries, when Paleopaganism was blending into Mesopaganism, or Mesopaganism into

Neopaganism. Furthermore, many of the founders and members of
Mesopagan or Neopagan groups prefer to believe (or at least declare)
that they are being genuinely Paleopagan—or genuinely Christian, in
the case of medieval Europeans—in their beliefs and practices. This
"myth of continuity" (as anthropologists call it) is in keeping with the
habits of most founders and members of new religions throughout
human existence. Indeed, as we shall see, Wicca's founding myths
very much included this idea of a continuous spiritual, if not historical, connection to previous generations of Pagan religious witches.

For the purposes of this book, we need to stress that the move
from Palepaganism to Christianity in Europe was particularly slow
and torturous (sometimes literally). History books will speak of particular parts of Europe as having been "converted" to Christianity in
particular years or decades, when all too often the conversions were
only skin deep, and only among the upper classes. Rather than thinking of a historical map of Europe showing blue Pagan "states" turning
into red Christian ones (as some members of the Religious Reich in
America might hope for our nation), let's use a more accurate visual
metaphor, since Paleopagan Europe didn't really have much in the
way of nation-states north of Rome.

Imagine a map of Europe around the beginning of the first century CE. There's a large spot of (let's make it orange) color with fuzzy
edges showing in Judea for the monotheistic Jews, with darker orange
areas for the Essenes and other mystical Jews. Elsewhere, tiny splashes
of checkered black and white (for the Zoroastrian dualists) overlap
some of the golden areas where the Pythagoreans and other Gnostics*
live in the cities around the rim of the Mediterranean. Everything else
is sky-blue Paleopaganism. During the first century CE, a reddish-
orange cult called the Nazereans appears in Judea, perhaps overlapping some of the dark orange spots; then dark red spots begin to
appear elsewhere, mostly in the Roman Empire's cities, heavily mixed
with orange, gold, and checks. In Judea, the red-orange is obliterated

*New Agers, more or less.

by dark red at about the time the surrounding orange is scattered throughout the Roman Empire (140 CE). During the rest of the second and third centuries CE, a dark-and-light checked red gradually replaces other color in the cities and begins to flow first into the local rural areas, then north, east, and west with the Roman Empire's troops.

Over the next few centuries, a red tinge turns the sky-blue of Hispania and Gaul purplish, then flows among the Germans and the island Celts. Dark red spots appear within the purple areas, as Paleopagan clergy are converted or killed and replaced, Paleopagan shrines and temples are destroyed, and Christian towns, cities, and abbeys are founded on the ruins. The process repeats among the Scandinavians, the eastern Europeans, the Slavs, and finally the Balts in the seventeenth century. In the vast majority of places, the purple remains in the rural regions, is replaced by light red in the small towns, and becomes dark blood red in the cities and political power centers. The popes and bishops (and their Protestant successors) congratulate themselves on the conquest of Pagandom by Christendom, but they have to keep a sharp eye on the ignorant and uneducated, who are still three-quarters (the rural ones) or half (the small-town ones) Pagan in their habits and beliefs—most of which the locals think are Christian! It will be among these rural and small-town Mesopagans that the vast majority of our different kinds of "witches," real and imaginary, will be found in the chapters that follow.

Such a color system could simultaneously describe the back-and-forth battle with the green of Islam (which gradually became light-and-dark checked by dualism as well) during the Crusades and afterward, and see its blue-green conquest of Spain, Africa, and parts of India. We could watch the more recent replacement of the remaining European purples and reds by waves of a new golden color coming from the cities during the Age of Enlightenment and the rise of modern science, even while the reds were frantically continuing to cast themselves into sky-blue Africa, Australia, and the Americas.

In fact, if I had the resources of a university department of religious studies, I would love to make a computer program that would map these religious migrations and conquests as flowing colors that blend with one another, rather than the deceptive solids that claim to depict religious evolution and contacts. The "all one color or the other" approach is rather dualistic—yet another example of the poisoned waters in which even fine academic minds swim all unknowing. However, I don't have a university job, so let's leave that programming task to someone else and move forward with the primary focus of this work: figuring out who the witches really were.

PART ONE

# PALEOPAGAN
# WITCHCRAFT

# CHAPTER 1

# What Does the Word "Witch" Mean?

"Who were the witches? Where did they come from?
Maybe your great-great-grandmother was one." *

r maybe not. These questions require complex answers, since during the centuries that the word has been known, it has had several definitions, including ones referring to the people described in the introduction. Even people who call themselves "witches" today, or who point to others as being such, differ widely in their interpretations of the term.

Is a "witch" anyone who does magic or who reads fortunes? Is a witch someone who worships the Christian Devil? Is a Witch (capital letter this time) a member of a specific faith called "Wicca"—and does he or she need to have been initiated as such by someone else? Is a witch someone who practices Voodoo, Macumba, or Candomble? Are anthropologists correct when they define a witch as anyone who is suspected of doing evil magic and/or of being a monster who can curse people with the "evil eye"? Were the first witches originally shamans munching on psychedelic herbs and mushrooms?

All these definitions have been claimed as accurate in the past and are used to this day by both friends and foes of whatever they think

*"Who Were the Witches?" © 2002 Bonnie Lockhart.

11

witchcraft might be. Most people discussing the topic seem to have their own pet definition and get very annoyed with those of differing opinions.

Is there a way out of this quagmire? Is it possible to distinguish between "real" and "fake" witches? Much of the evidence that would enable us to give positive answers to the relevant questions was deliberately suppressed or destroyed centuries ago by those with religious, economic, and/or political axes to grind. Yet, as this book will show, we *can* construct a reasonably good picture of all the different kinds of witches (real and imaginary) by considering the surviving historical, linguistic, mythological, and folkloric evidence. Let's start with a little linguistic material.*

As many people now know, the word "witch" in Modern English comes from the Old English *wicce* (probably pronounced "wich-" as in sandwich,† plus "-eh"), which was the feminine noun and *wicca* ("wich-ah,"), which was the masculine. The plural noun was *wiccan*‡ ("wich-an"). These Old English words referred to agents or performers of *wiccian* ("wich-en"), which may have meant sorcery or magic in general, or just "what witches do" with multiple connotations. These *wic-* words came from one or more of a cluster of similar-sounding (and easily confused both then and now) Germanic and (going further back into history) Proto-Indo-European (PIE) linguistic roots (see below and appendix 1). These PIE roots (variations of *weg-* and *weik-)*, and the early words that grew out of them and then became the roots of later words, seemed to have referred to related concepts of waking, shouting, bending, weaving, changing, turning, twisting, and willows and items made out of them (such as wicker-work).

So the Paleo- and Mesopagan Indo-European (see below) cultures, like most others before and since, associated the concepts of speech,

---

*I know that many people are bugged by etymology (the study of word origins and histories), so before people get antsy, I have put most of the formidable details into appendix 1.

†Pronouncing the "ch" the same way the British say the "t" in "tune."

‡Now used with a capital letter (and pronounced "Wik-en") as an adjective for followers of Neopagan Witchcraft (see part three).

intention, and the performance of magic, and at least some of the
time expressed these ideas in terms of bending, twisting, and weaving.* All those concepts could have had magical implications and applications for the people using them. However, since some of these
similar-sounding roots referred to people or things that were weak/
wicked, pliable (the willow connection again), unimportant, or mean
(of low social class), they might tend to be used mostly when talking
about negative or low-class magic.

This is all very suggestive, but to attempt to determine exactly
what the earliest people using the *wic-* words thought of the people
they called "witches" and the activity they called "witchcraft," we will
need a bridge between linguistic and cultural information.

You may already know that linguists divide human languages into
language "families" of related tongues. Irish, Manx, and Scots Gaelic,
for example, along with Welsh, Cornish, and Breton, are called the
Goidelic and Brittonic branches, respectively, of the Insular (island)
Celtic language family. Add Gaulish and Celtiberian, together called
Continental Celtic, and you get the larger Celtic family. Add the
Celtic to the Italic, Germanic, and Balto-Slavic languages, and you
get the Western and Northern branches of the larger Indo-European
(IE) language family. English, by the way, started out as a Germanic
tongue, spoken by the people we now call the Anglo-Saxons.
Sanskrit, another related tongue, was spoken in Vedic India (2000
BCE through 1000 CE), hence the "Indo" in Indo-European.

All the IE languages are considered to have descended from the
partially reconstructed PIE language spoken thousands of years ago
in or near what is now Turkey.† After several millennia of technologi-

*Such as the old Irish stories of spells being cast by the use of bent and woven
saplings carved with ogham letters.
†As demonstrated in *The Origin of Language: Tracing the Evolution of the Mother
Tongue* by Merritt Ruhlen. By presenting exercises the readers can perform, the author is able to show that all human languages come from one African original
tongue and that the PIE language spread from Anatolia/Turkey, along with the
technology of agriculture, beginning around 7000–6500 BCE. His work fits almost
perfectly with the results of genetic database analysis of human migrations.

cal adoption, migration, conquest, and intermarriage, the speakers of
the various IE languages now dominate much of the globe. Certainly,
their cultures controlled most of Europe during the times when Old
English was being spoken and *wicce/wicca* was being used to describe
people.

The social anthropologist and folklorist Georges Dumézil discovered in the early twentieth century that the religious beliefs and cos-
mologies (ideas about the nature of the universe), as well as certain
social and technological assumptions and descriptions, that were em-
bedded in the myths of the different IE-speaking peoples were analo-
gous to each other and more or less to the same degree that their
languages shared similarities in word sounds, grammar, and vocabulary. After all, one of the major uses of language is to tell stories,
whether about deities or ancestors, and these stories would be carried
along with the rest of a language as it traveled or mutated. Thus, similar characters going through similar plotlines could be seen in Celtic,
Germanic, Roman, Greek, Hittite, and Vedic myths. Of the many
cultural aspects shared by the Indo-Europeans, I believe the ones related to social structures are directly connected to understanding the
original role of people we might think of as "witches" in their communities, if only by the witches' absence in most of the older tales.

IE tribes usually had a chieftain (or more rarely a chieftainess)* as
the center of a series of concentric circles of power and influence.
There was a class of intellectuals (Dumézil's "first function" of judi-
cial/educational and magical power), a class of warriors (his "second
function" of force and protection), a class of producers (his "third
function" of food and craft support), a class of servants or slaves (a
"fourth function" of necessary dirty work), and a vague ("fifth function"?) category of "weirdos" and "outsiders" (everyone else from village eccentrics, to traveling merchants, to itinerant entertainers, to
the tribe three mountains away).† All these classes of humans, along

---

*Usually referred to as a king or queen in translations of the stories.
†Alwyn Rees and Brinley Rees's *Celtic Heritage*, an early and now classic book
applying Dumézil's theories of Irish and Welsh mythology, sparked much of my

with deities, other spirits, and the forces of nature, could be described as belonging to two categories of "light" and "dark," corresponding to safe and dangerous, or sometimes to appropriate and inappropriate, examples of each category.* I believe that each of the social classes or castes was divided into subcastes reflecting the others, just as the "Three Worlds" of the Land, the Waters, and the Sky (three places one finds living beings) were reflected in the myths into the Cythonic (underground), the Middle, and the Celestial Realms.†

What's important for our discussion here is the intellectual class and its divisions. Among the Celtic peoples, this was the "druid" class, among the Germanic peoples, the "godi" class, among the Italic peoples, the "flamen" class, among the Vedic peoples, the "brahman" class, and so on. The people who acted as priests or priestesses (and therefore magicians as well) were members of this class, along with seers, sacrificers, judges, historians, poets, and musicians—anyone who worked primarily with his or her mind. A druid as such, for example, would be the one leading public rituals that the entire tribe depended on, while a seer or sacrificer would be a second-function person within the first function, because his or her activities were ones dealing with death and the dead, like the activities of the warriors. A bard or poet would be a third-function person within the first function and the stable hands who took care of the sacred animals to be sacrificed would be the fourth-function people within the first function. A traveling judge or visiting priestess would perhaps be a first-of-first functionary in his or her home tribe and a fifth-of-first functionary in all the other tribes on his or her route.

---

speculations on this with their discussion of the "Five Provinces" of ancient Ireland and Wales—one of which was a center (corresponding to the king), three of which corresponded to the "important" three functions, and one which was divided in two (corresponding to my suggested fourth and fifth functions).

*It was Zoroaster who decided that "light and dark" meant "absolute good and evil," thus creating the dualism that was to poison Western cultures for 2,500 years.

†See *Bonewits's Essential Guide to Druidism* and the works of Dumézil listed in appendix 5.

So where are the witches in this picture? I suspect they were on the outside looking in. Theoretically, they could have been thought of as "dark/dangerous magicians" within the first function, as the much-feared satirists (composers and reciters of satirical poetry and songs) were as "dark poets" among the druids. Or they might have been a reflection of the first function within the fourth function or within the fifth-function outsiders (see below). But while the first four functions were associated (in their light sides at least) with cosmic order, most outsiders (light or dark) were associated with chaos. The intellectuals, and therefore their cultures as a whole, were obsessed with the topics of order and chaos, considering the first to be much better than the second, and spent a great deal of their time and energy attempting to maintain order from the cosmic to the tribal levels, especially through their maintenance of ritual and cultural continuity from generation to generation. In fact, the word "druid" comes from a Celtic root *dru- (from the PIE root *deru- or *dreu-, the source of many words meaning firmness, stability, truth, trees, and wood—especially oak), plus the Celtic *wid- (from the PIE *weid-), usually said to mean one who sees (physically or spiritually). The warriors and others who dealt with death seem to have been associated with yew trees or other evergreens, the producers with birches, and the servants/slaves with beeches.*

By contrast, the tree most associated in myth and history with witchcraft seems to have been the willow (PIE *wy-, which might be a source of the *weg- and *weik- mentioned earlier). Perhaps the willow-like "bending" and "chaos" of wiccecraeft ("witchcraft") and the oak-like "firmness" and "order" of draíocht ("druidry") may correlate with an ancient distinction between the social functions played by each.† Just as a seer could be seen as a reflection of the warrior class

---

*No doubt leading to arguments about whether the offspring of unknown fathers were "sons of birches" or "sons of beeches."

†See *Proto-Indo-European Trees* by Paul Freidrich for more on the tree connections and *The New Comparative Mythology* by C. Scott Littleton and *The Plight of a Sorcerer* by Georges Dumézil for more on the clergy caste.

within the clergy class, and a bard as a reflection of the producer class within the clergy, so *perhaps* a person of the sort I call a "Classic Witch" (see next chapter) could have been seen as a reflection of the clergy/intelligentsia class within the servant or outsider classes, because they were knowledge-workers. There is little, however, in the linguistic origins of *wiccel/wicca* to indicate an ancient *religious* role for witches except possibly as symbols or representatives of the energies of chaos. Like all IE cultures, the Germanic tongues (from which Old English sprang) had specific words for "priest," "priestess," "healer," "midwife," "matchmaker," "advisor," and "wise one"—few of which appear to have been linguistically related to the various words that became *wiccel/wicca* in Old English.

Even at the height of the witch-hunting hysteria in the late Middle Ages and Renaissance, the terms used outside England to refer to the victims—such as *fascinatrix* (binder), *herbaria* (herbalist), *Hexen* (magician), and *Wettermacherinnen* (weatherworker)—all meant people (usually women) with real or assumed herbal, magical, and prophetic knowledge or powers, who were believed to be able to control people, raise storms, and kill or cure. As far as I know, it was only in Ireland (where the persecutions were comparatively mild) that the specifically religious term *bandraoi* (druidess) was used, along with others such as *cailleich* (hag/old woman) and *bean feasa* (woman of knowledge) to refer to the people others elsewhere were calling witches. By then, *draíocht*, which used to just mean druidical arts of all sorts, had come in Ireland to mean "magic" in general, so it is anyone's guess as to how much of the previous religious meanings were left when an Irish person in the 1400s called someone else a druid or druidess.

So, despite the modern Wiccan belief that *wicca* originally meant "wise one," what it really meant was a combination of one or more of the following ideas: (1) someone who could bend things to his or her will, (2) someone who could turn aside good or evil (and thus bless or curse you), (3) someone who could (magically) "wake the dead" and presumably get information from them, (4) someone who could cast spells, and (5) someone of a weak or immoral character, (6) usually of a lower class than the speaker of the term. Here is what is important about all this: *the people we could call the Original Witches\* were probably called witches by others, not themselves, and the terms used for them had neutral-to-negative connotations even among the Paleopagans.*

The "wise one" derivation may have been suggested to Gerald Gardner, the creator of Wicca as a religion (see chapter 8), by one or more of the following factors (1) the word *wica,* which *may* have meant "wise"; (2) he might have been thinking of the word *wysard* (or "wizard"), which *does* mean "wise one" and which was used in the Renaissance as a term for a male witch after the masculine form of *wicca* had been forgotten; and/or (3) the "cunning folk" who throughout English history were sometimes called witches and sometimes wizards and who provided some of the folk magic Gardner incorporated into his religion.

But whatever else they may have been, Paleopagan witches were *not* usually the priests and priestesses of "The Old Religion" (as if there had ever been only one) of ancient Europe, despite such claims by many modern Wiccans. While I can imagine a druid or godi being called a witch during a particularly nasty argument, it would have been an insult to be long remembered.

What happened after the original Pagan clergy (the druids, godis, flamens, etc.) were wiped out by the Roman Empire and/or the Christian Church? Did the people once called witches fill a power vacuum left by them? To find out, we will have to look at the people I've called the Classic Witches.

---

\*Or the *urhexen* if we want to get really scholarly about it!

# CHAPTER 2

# Classic Witches as Cunning Folk

he image of witches that many people (especially Wiccans) have matches the old lady in her cottage with the two cauldrons, whom we met in the introduction. Much of this image comes from fairy tales and legends, rather than from history, but it is a fairly clear picture of people I called, in earlier editions of this work, "Classic Witches."

These people still existed as recently as the middle of the twentieth century in England and Europe, especially in the areas where modern science was slow to replace folk beliefs. These people were usually referred to in their local languages as "cunning," "clever," or sometimes "wise" men and women—at least to their faces. Their activities included healing (with medicines and/or magic), sometimes midwifery, and the related skills of inducing fertility (and abortions). Other areas of expertise that some might have included were providing love potions (and poisons), predicting and/or controlling the weather, blessing (and cursing), fortune-telling, and discovering witches who might have hexed their clients. Most of these people did not call themselves witches (except when they wanted to scare people), even though their enemies might have done so behind their backs or nostalgic Wiccans might do so now.

For our purposes here, we shall define a Classic Witch (or "cunning man/woman") as follows: a person (usually an older female)

who is adept in the uses of herbs, roots, barks, and so on for the purposes of both healing and hurting people, animals, or crops (including the making of poisons, aphrodisiacs, hallucinogens, etc.), who is
familiar with the basic principles of both passive (receptive/divina-
tory) and active (spell-casting) magic,* and who can use them for
good or ill—as she or he chooses. Note that this is an idealized, almost fantasy, image, as many cunning folk (to judge from research by
folklorists of the last couple of centuries and medieval trial records)
might only know a handful of spells or understand how to cure three
or four illnesses. Based on my current research about such people as
being more enemies of criminal witches than witches themselves, I'm
going to refer to these classic witches mostly under the more accurate
term of "cunning folk" for the majority of this edition.†

A typical cunning woman or man, being an old peasant, might
also be filled with country wisdom and superstitions and be a shrewd
judge of character. She or he might be a midwife, barber/surgeon,
blacksmith, or just another farmer in the village. Such a person would
be of great value to local peasants, but would also be somewhat frightening and resented. The old woman living on the edge of the village
(because the villagers drove her there, see chapter 4) with her garden
of herbs and collection of old sayings and incantations really existed,
unlike some of the other kinds of witches we'll be meeting. And as we
shall see, a few of them wound up on the wrong side of the local laws.

But what had the cunning folk done when Pagan priests and
priestesses were still around? Remembering that almost everyone in a
Paleopagan culture will do simple folk magic for him- or herself, did
the cunning folk exist side by side with the clergy, handling simple or
private (or unethical?) matters while the clergy handled complicated
or public ones? That doesn't seem too unlikely, but perhaps the cunning folk only began to exist as an occupation after the clergy had
been overthrown, because they *were* the unconverted remnants of

---

*See my book *Real Magic*.
†And this is how I dance away from my previous usages of the term!☺

that clergy and their descendants, looked on with both nostalgia and distrust. Nobody really knows, though lots of people have theories.

There do seem to have been Paleopagan religious communities of both genders in Celtic territories, perhaps similarly patterned to ones in India formed in the woods (then and now) by retired householders who have left their previous castes and duties behind.* The communities for Celtic women have been described as being situated on islands surrounded by willow trees that, as mentioned earlier, were the trees most associated with chaos and witches (and most likely to be found around islands, since willows grow best near water). There were also individual mystics living solitary lives in the woods, perhaps similar to the *arhats* (saints) of India. Some priestesses of Freya in the ninth century CE in parts of Scandinavia, for example, lived as solitary mystics, minding small temples and riding from village to village with statues of Freya for rituals at various times of the year. Could some of the cunning folk have been descended from such communities or individuals? Maybe. We will probably never know for sure. If they did, it would support the "magical person at the edge of the woods" part of the image of the classic witch.

So to answer the question asked at the end of the previous chapter, the criminal witches *might* have filled any power vacuums left by a local loss of the Paleopagan clergy, but the cunning folk would have been in a better social position to do so (being more trusted) and they would have been competing with the new Christian clergy for magical customers.

While the classic witch in its archetypal power is usually female, another image, one we could call the Classic Wizard, is usually male. Where does it come from? The term "wise one" (Old English *wysard*) could have been merely a compliment, applied to anyone showing extraordinary wisdom about a topic—even today it is used that way

---

*This is one of several examples of a cultural equivalent to the linguistic principle called "fossilization at the extremes," with a particular religious custom rather than a fragment of vocabulary or syntax being the item that survives at the furthest reaches of a language family's spread.

in such phrases as "computer wizard." However, contrary to the beliefs of many occultists and theologians, wisdom never has been limited strictly to people involved in magical and religious occupations.

A classic wizard is usually described as a loner, a stranger who wan-
ders about performing wondrous deeds with little equipment save a
staff or sword. In fact, the description is very similar to that found in
the *Eddas* of the Norse God Odin as He walks about the earth. Odin
is associated with the dark/dangerous half of the IE first-function
caste of judges/historians and magicians/priests. Could it be that the
term *wysard* became attached to various Pagan priests who had gone
into hiding and who perhaps traveled from village to village, providing some of their old priestly services to people now no longer able to
get them? Us romantics would love to believe it.* Or were wizards
really just what they called some of the male cunning folk, much of
whose business was undoing the supposed curses of witches? And
could the same person find himself being called a criminal witch if
something went wrong?

I suspect that the greatest influence on what modern people think
of wizards as having been was J.R.R. Tolkien, who created his famous
wizard, Gandalf, based in large part on Odin. One of Gandalf's
names was Mithrandir, which means "Gray Wanderer," one of Odin's
titles. A thousand fantasy novels launched by Tolkien's success created
a thousand other wizards, each more fascinating than the previous,†
each further away from historical reality. As much as we might love
them, they really don't have much to do with the real history of
witchcraft (except at Hogwarts).

Neither do shamans, though they have been dragged into the discussion repeatedly over the last few decades. So let's divert the stream
of this discussion for a chapter about them.

---

*Hence, my song, "The Bard's Lament."
†My favorite is Terry Pratchett's character Rincewind. See my recent work, *The
Pagan Man,* for more about ancient and modern wizards.

CHAPTER 3

# Gonna Take a
# Shamanistic Journey . . .

ost Westerners became aware of shamans and their beliefs and practices when Mircea Eliade published his
classic *Shamanism: Archaic Techniques of Ecstasy* in 1951.*
As he described it, "shamanism" was a complex but clear
cluster of phenomena, involving people who performed particular
kinds of magical and religious rituals within a specific cultural context.

Paleopagan shamans were:

(1) tribal officials in
(2) hunter-gatherer cultures who
(3) were usually reluctant recruits who
(4) underwent a harrowing death and rebirth experience that
(5) enabled them to leave their bodies at will while
(6) deities, ancestors, or other spirits possessed them and/or
(7) they traveled to other worlds to
(8) represent their tribe to the deities (asking for help or blessings) and/or
(9) to find and return the errant souls of sick members of their
tribe.

*First in French, then in English in 1964.

Eliade asserted further that most shamans:

(10)  were from Northern, Central, or Eastern Asian cultures (or
among their distant relations, the Native Americans),

(11)  shared a particular form of "x-ray art" that showed animal
skeletons inside their bodies,

(12)  often used sleight of hand in their healing magic,

(13)  and sometimes used drumming and/or mind-altering substances as aids to inducing trances and leaving their bodies.

In 1968, Carlos Castaneda began publishing a striking series of
fantasy novels that he successfully passed off as anthropological research for many years about a Native American shaman named Don
Juan, who supposedly taught him all about the magical and spiritual
uses of peyote, datura, and funny mushrooms.

In 1973, Michael Harner said in a book he edited, *Hallucinogens
and Shamanism,* that the "flying ointments" referred to in many
medieval documents as having been used by witches seem to have
regularly contained various hallucinogenic herbs such as belladonna,
henbane, datura, and so on, which can in combination produce illu-
sions of flying as well as visions of wild orgies and dancing.

In 1974, Morning Glory Zell-Ravenheart (1948– ) pointed out
that users of belladonna around the world frequently reported seeing
the same "White Lady," Whom they associated with various moon
and sea goddesses, just as users of peyote from different cultures often
seemed to meet the same green vegetation deity, most commonly
known as "San Mescalito." She felt it possible that independent cults
of belladonna users worshipping this common White Lady could
have sprung up in multiple parts of Paleopagan Europe and that they
might have survived here and there into the Middle Ages, only to be
persecuted by the Church. She called this idea of Pagan belladonna
cultists "Shamanic Witchcraft," because of the then increasingly
common (and false) assumption that shamanism was mostly a matter
of the ritual use of hallucinogens.

However, according to Taylor Ellwood, author of *Pop Culture Magick* and (with D. M. Cunningham and T. A. R. Wagener) *Creating Magickal Entities*, different brain chemicals may indeed generate perceptions of (themselves as?) anthropomorphic entities within the human mind. He tells me that he did a series of experiments with a colleague, Zac Walters, and others to determine how different neurotransmitters might be perceived as entities.

His method involved using Austin Osman Spare's "Alphabet of Desire" (a way of creating magical symbols to be used as talismans), as well as a combination of John Lilly's theories on "programming the human biocomputer" and Barbara Ann Brennan's approach of narrowing the consciousness down to a cell so as to travel into the body. Taylor used these approaches to devise a meditational vision quest where he would journey into his body and find a specific neurotransmitter and the entity that embodied it.

Once contact was made with an entity, a symbol for the Alphabet of Desire was required and then used in subsequent journeys to both contact the neurotransmitter entity and strengthen that connection, as well as inducing altered states of mind consistent with results that would occur if the neurotransmitter was overly stimulated. Zac Walters also began using this technique, after learning about it from Taylor Ellwood. They did their work mostly independently but occasionally shared results, which ended up with some intriguing further results. Both participants found that the neurotransmitters occupied similar roles in terms of archetypal characteristics. For example, dopamine was the Trickster for both of them. Although not all of their descriptions were similar, in some cases, such as with melatonin, a similar name and appearance was found by both independently of each other.

The two did further experiments to determine the role neurotransmitters have in the effectiveness of magical workings. Zac Walters surmised that high levels of serotonin could be responsible for such phenomena as astral projection (out of the body experiences). Both he and Taylor, as well as several others, took turns alternating between a tryptophan heavy diet (which produces serotonin) and bombarding

themselves with heavy amounts of florescent light, followed by days
with neither exposure. It did seem that the astral projections were
more likely to occur on the tryptophan heavy days or the light bom-
bardment days.*

What is intriguing about this admittedly "amateur" research (nobody was paying them to do it) is that the participants repeatedly
found out that the magical law of personification ("Anything can be a
person") seemed to naturally apply itself to internally perceived entities and that specific brain chemicals seemed to be associated with
similar appearing entities. Since different mind altering substances
produce different combinations of brain chemicals, Morning Glory
Zell might have been onto something back in the 1970s.

Throughout the 1970s and '80s, books about the spirituality of
hallucinogens met an eager market. Castaneda kept cranking out
more novels, later Lynne Andrews and other New Age authors began
telling similar tales, and Harner published books about shamans in
the Amazon jungle. Together, these authors essentially redefined
shamanism as any system of magic or religion that used mind-altering
substances—which is, of course, most of them at one time or another. Eliade's once-clear definition became lost in a psychedelic
cloud of vague generalities.

In the 1980s and '90s, others were to call their new versions of
Wicca (or Neopagan Witchcraft—see part three) Shamanic Wicca,
even though these others did not advocate or use psychedelics in their
worship. They did, however, wave feathers and crystals around (as
they had been told shamans did) and pound on drums a lot, so they
figured that was close enough to shamanism.

It seems clear to me that classic witches/cunning folk (not to mention the imaginary Diabolic Witches to be discussed in chapter 4) fulfilled almost none of the characteristics Eliade outlined as essential to
shamanism. Let's do it by the numbers:

---

*Taylor Ellwood details more about this work in his forthcoming book *Inner
Alchemy.*

1. They weren't tribal officials; they were marginal members of their villages, when not actually outcasts (unless we go with the idea that some of them were the remnants of the former Pagan clergy).

2. They lived in or on the outskirts of settled agricultural societies, rather than within hunter-gatherer ones, which had been gone from most of Europe for centuries by the time the cunning folk enter history—the Indo-Europeans brought agriculture, remember?

3. Cunning folk sometimes served apprenticeships with older cunning folk, but there is little to suggest that they usually resisted becoming such. Most seem to have stumbled into the role as a hobby or an additional possible source of income.

4. The death and rebirth experience crucial to the initiation of a shaman is simply absent from the life stories of people we know of as cunning folk, although it is interesting that some cunning folk, like some modern psychics, did have severe injuries or illnesses as children. It was sometimes said that accused Diabolic Witches had been painfully raped by the Devil and/or "baptized" into his service, but that's a far cry from having every single bit of flesh and nerve stripped from your bones, as shamanic initiates report.

5. There is very little evidence that soul travel ("astral projection" or "out of body experiences" as modern occultists and parapsychologists, respectively, refer to it) was a major part of what cunning folk did.* Ironically, however, this was part of what the Diabolic Witches and their foes the *benedanti* of Italy supposedly did (see chapter 4).

6. Trance possession by deities or other spirits, central to the shamanic profession, isn't mentioned in connection with the cunning folk until after some of them began to practice Spiritualistic mediumship in the late nineteenth century.

*Despite evidence of bardic training among the druids having involved out-of-body experiences.

7. The closest thing to descriptions of "traveling to other worlds" that cunning folk might have done can be found in medieval tales of bards and others stumbling into the realm of Faerie. I suppose we could consider the sabbats of the supposed Diabolic Witches to have happened in another world, as the described activities would have been most unlikely in this one, but the switch from being considered "Classic" to being "Diabolic" happened to only a minority of the cunning folk.

8. I am aware of zero evidence that the cunning folk were considered to be speakers for their communities to deities or other spirits, except for their frequent custom of performing pilgrimages for individual clients to Christian holy sites dedicated to specific saints.

9. Neither do we have evidence of cunning folk working to find and return sick people's "missing" souls as part of their healing practices.

10. Western Europe certainly wasn't part of Northern, Central, or Eastern Asia or the Americas, although the Scandinavian cunning folk may have picked up techniques from the Finnish and Sami/Lapp peoples, who were members of Northern Asian cultures and did practice shamanism well into modern times. Central and eastern Europeans similarly could have been influenced by the Central Asian cultures.

11. X-ray art is conspicuous by its absence in medieval and early modern Europe.

12. Sleight of hand is mentioned in modern writing about cunning folk, but it is also common all over the world among folk magicians and healers, so it isn't particularly unique to shamans.

13. Drumming and drugs are also commonly used by magicians, healers, and clergy around the world to induce trances, so the use of either or both by either criminal witches or cunning folk isn't proof of shamanism or shamanic influences. In fact,

drumming isn't mentioned much, if at all, in medieval records
about cunning folk and the herbal drugs described as used by
them were usually given to patients or victims, not taken by
the cunning folk themselves.

The bottom line? It is unlikely that either the classic witches/cun-
ning folk, or any of the other witches in this book, were the remnants
of pre-Christian shamanism surviving underground inside Christendom
(see chapter 5 for some comments on underground religions). Ironically, the benedanti of medieval Italy (also chapter 5), which started
out as a cult dedicated to *fighting* criminal witches in a spirit world,
may have been the closest to matching Morning Glory's original concept of Shamanic Witchcraft.

If you are interested in learning about real shamanism, I would
strongly suggest that you first read Eliade's *Shamanism,* then go to a
university or college with an anthropology library and read what it
has on the topic before (if ever) going on to the more popular New
Age titles. Then you can decide if you really want to experience having your body torn to shreds by spirit animals and then painfully reconstructed, before dedicating the rest of your life to helping a
particular community with all their physical and psychic health problems as well as hunting and fishing luck.

PART TWO

# MESOPAGAN WITCHCRAFT

CHAPTER 4

# Imaginary Diabolic Witches and the "Burning Times"

erforming folk magic, whether as an amateur or as one of the cunning folk, wasn't actually a crime during the early centuries of the Christian era, nor was it even considered very sinful. Someone confessing to have cast spells could be expected to be given a few weeks or months of "penance," such as fasting and prayers, or perhaps be told to go on a pilgrimage to a local holy site. On subsequent occasions, or if someone was a well-known/notorious cunning person or accused of the criminal use of magic, the penances might be made increasingly severe, but when the Church was controlling witchcraft trials in the early Middle Ages, only a small fraction of accused criminal witches were executed.* The Church had bigger fish to fry, such as heretics and recalcitrant Pagans, and was more interested in bringing the stray sheep back to the flock then in killing half of them. As for the secular authorities, it was only if someone was suspected of having caused actual physical damages that he or she would be prosecuted, and then it was for having caused harm, not for doing magic.

Indeed, for a while it was official Church policy that all the magic produced by non-Christians was "illusionary" or "demonic" and that the belief in the ability of anyone to fly through the air, cast spells,

---

*Here, as throughout the following centuries, we cannot count the numbers who were lynched by angry mobs without the Church or the state ever hearing about it until afterward.

and so on was a Pagan and "therefore" heretical belief. An official Church document on this was the *Canon Episcopi* (*Law of the Church*), which was purported to be from the fourth century, but was (according to Rossell Hope Robbins) actually forged by a Churchman around 906 CE. This, in Robbins's translation in his *Encyclopedia of Witchcraft and Demonology*, read in part:

> It is also not to be admitted that certain abandoned women perverted by Satan, seduced by illusions and phantasms of demons, believe and openly profess that, in the dead of night, they ride upon certain beasts with the pagan goddess Diana, with a countless horde of women, and in the silence of the dead of night fly over vast tracts of country, and obey her commands as their mistress, while they are summoned to her service on other nights.
>
> But it were well if they alone perished in their infidelity and did not draw so many others along with them into the pit of their faithlessness. For an innumerable multitude, deceived by this false opinion, believe this to be true and, so believing, wander from the right faith and relapse into pagan errors when they think that there be any divinity or power except the one God.
>
> . . . It is therefore to be publicly proclaimed to all, that whoever believes such things or similar things loses the faith.

Note the phrase "when they think that there be any divinity or power except the one God." Non-Church magic was officially impossible and the magic that the priests and monks of the Church did— which was never to be called magic—was the only real kind. So people believing in folk magic, even when it invoked the deities of Christianity, were being both foolish and un-Christian. This was the official party line for several centuries and caused theological trouble later when the Church wanted to persecute people for doing what Church doctrine had earlier said was impossible.

The *Canon Episcopi*'s indication, coming as late as 906, that the Church was aware of Pagan survivals in its heartland of Italy (assuming that it meant the ancient Roman Diana, and not another goddess of similar nature) was taken by some writers in the mid-twentieth century as evidence for theories that the great witch hunts were "really" aimed at an underground Pagan cult of Diana worshipers (see chapter 5). However, it proves nothing except that there were at least a few Mesopagan beliefs connected with women's religious behavior in Christendom—something we know from other sources as well.

When the *Canon Episcopi* was announced in the early tenth century, there were still unconverted Paleopagans in northern and eastern Europe building temples, carving statues of their gods, giving sacrifices to trees and streams, and so on. There were survivals of similar behavior throughout western Europe, for an Anglo-Saxon law of about the same time condemns supposed (criminal) witches for worshiping wells, trees, stones, and so on. This seems to indicate that for several centuries after the Christian conquest of southern and western Europe, at least some of the people who were called "witches" were only mildly Christianized. This law isn't evidence of an organized cult of witches in Anglo-Saxon territory, however, nor are the worship activities mentioned in it part of the twentieth-century theories of how a postulated cult of witches worshiped, factors that will become important as we go along further in our discussion.

How did people normally become accused of criminal witchcraft? Robin Briggs shows us in her groundbreaking work *Witches and Neighbors*. Someone in the village or who lived a few doors down the block in your small town might come by to borrow a bit of milk or flour, be refused, then walk away mumbling. A few hours or days later, you, your child, or your cow might become sick or even die— the would-be borrower must have been a criminal witch who cast a spell out of spite! Or a beggar would come up to you in the street, be refused alms, and then loudly wish you to become as poor as he. Any subsequent bad luck resulting in financial losses could then be laid at the criminal witch's feet.

The psychological mechanisms are fairly simple: they are a variation of survivor's guilt. Most people in southern and western Europe in the Middle Ages were poor. During and after the pandemic of the Black Death (1347–49), this poverty became much worse and social bonds were strained to the breaking point. People could barely manage to provide for their own and their children's needs, let alone help others. But Christian doctrine and Pagan custom alike, rooted in the same need to create and maintain social bonds, required people to be generous and charitable, even when it was difficult. So refusing to give milk to a woman for her starving children or a small coin to a homeless beggar, then as now, made the better-off person feel guilty. The obvious way (that doesn't cost anything) to get rid of the guilt is to blame the borrower or beggar for his or her own situation.* You can declare that they are drunkards, sluts, or (should you have bad luck shortly after refusing charity) criminal witches.

This was complicated by the fact that many accused criminal witches would be persuaded (gently or roughly) to heal their "victims," as it was thought that only the witch who had hexed someone could cure that person. Coming up with a successful cure might get one off the hook temporarily, but was liable to be brought up again years later (people in small towns have *long* memories). This "curser's cure" idea was one reason why a cunning person who couldn't figure out how to heal a client or his livestock would claim that the illness was due to a criminal witch's curse and turn the client's mind toward thinking of who might have cursed him.

By the eleventh century CE, any cunning folk who might have been consciously worshipping Pagan deities in the Church's territory had pretty much died out or were adding lots of Christian prayers to their activities. Most of the Paleopagan cultures of western and central Europe had been destroyed, and pacification programs had been instituted against any remaining objectors. Having slain all the avail-

*This is still the way that most Republicans treat the homeless in twenty-first-century America. Should the homeless refugees from the Gulf Coast cities hit by Hurricane Katrina in August 2005 remain homeless, the Republican-controlled government may have to come up with a different approach from simply ignoring and/or blaming these victims.

able competition outside of the Church, the Christians proceeded to alternate missionary pushes with slaying each other. The Holy Office of the Inquisition (those who inquire) was founded with the intent of investigating suspected un-Christian activities and Crusades were mounted against groups of "heretics" (*heresia*—one who "chooses" to believe something other than official Church doctrine). These were much more successful than the Crusades against the Moslems, who had the rude habit of winning. One of them, against a group called the Cathars in the thirteenth century, managed to murder every living speaker of the Oc language in France.

Heretic roasting became a lucrative source of wealth, power, and sexual satisfaction for both the Inquisitors and their civilian helpers. Eventually, however, they began to run out of heretics to kill. This was disastrous for them, since many inquisitors and nobles had built their fortunes on confiscated property taken from their victims. A few hopeful sadists, however, had been suggesting to the popes for quite some time that criminal witchcraft should be declared seriously heretical, rather than just unlawful. This was done slowly over a period of two centuries. As Jenny Gibbons says:

> Traditional attitudes towards witchcraft began to change in the 14th century, at the very end of the Middle Ages. As Carlo Ginzburg noted (*Ecstasies: Deciphering the Witches' Sabbat*), early 14th century central Europe was seized by a series of rumor-panics. Some malign conspiracy (Jews and lepers, Moslems, or Jews and witches) was attempting to destroy the Christian kingdoms through magick and poison. After the terrible devastation caused by the Black Death (1347–1349) these rumors increased in intensity and focused primarily on witches and "plague-spreaders."*

In 1324, Bernard Gui wrote a manual for heretic hunters that strongly influenced later ones, explaining what to look for and what

---

*See appendix 8, *"Recent Developments in the Study of the Great European Witch Hunt,"* by Jenny Gibbons.

questions to ask when ferreting out heresy. In 1376, Nicholas Eymeric published a similar popular handbook for inquisitors, which was in use through the end of the fifteenth century. In 1428, the Church created a six-point definition of a particular heresy in Calais and Arras (France) that was to eventually be used in a new definition of "witchcraft."*

The victims there were tortured until they confessed to:

1. Making a pact (a legal agreement) with the Christian Devil
2. Having sex with the Christian Devil
3. Flying around at night (as in the *Canon Episcopi*) with the Christian Devil
4. Working magic
5. Attending secret meetings at night
6. Being sexually promiscuous (having more sex than the inquisitors were)

In 1484, Pope Innocent VIII issued a papal bull officially sanctioning the arrest and trial (that is to say, the torture, conviction, and execution) of anyone accused of such consorting with demons. Soon after, two Catholic priests, Heinrich Kramer and James Sprenger, wrote and published (with the pope's approval or "*Imprimatur*") one of the more infamous books in history, the *Malleus Maleficarum* (*The Hammer of [Female] Evildoers*; which Montague Summers translated as *The Witches' Hammer*). While this may not have been as popular a book as Summers would have us believe, it was used along with the previous inquisitorial manuals (and a few later ones) to guide and justify 300 years of atrocities committed against women, children, and men for the thought-crime of worshipping the Christian Devil.

The theological excuses were easy to manufacture and were de-

*The Wiccan author Gavin Frost points out that limiting the term "witch trials" to only those cases involving these six particular characteristics is one way in which the numbers of those killed for witchcraft can be limited to the lower estimates— but see the discussion of body counts later on.

fended in Church literature well into the mid-twentieth century.* Since there was only "one God, one Faith, and one Church," anyone disagreeing with the Roman Catholic Church (or the later Protestant Churches) about anything was automatically a heretic. By similar dualistic reasoning, anyone using a system of magic outside of Christian control and approval was "obviously" doing it with the help of the Christian Devil. Satan was, after all, the only other god allowed to exist in Christian mythology—though they killed you if you called him one. Since the Christian Devil supposedly would not give magical power to people who weren't "his own," accused witches, including anyone accused of malevolent magic, "must" therefore have been worshiping him.

Many of the early Christian "heresies" had threatened the theological and political power of the bishop of Rome, who was now called the pope. The popes were especially sensitive on this matter, since most of the non-Roman bishops considered the popes to be heretics themselves, who had unlawfully usurped the powers of the early Christian Council of Bishops by declaring themselves solely in charge of the Church.†

Having crushed all opposition and declared their opponents to be the ones who were "really" the heretics, the bishops of Rome grabbed for all the religious and secular power they could get. Thus, as I often say, the Roman Empire never actually fell—it just changed hands and continued under new management!

Wherever the Roman Catholic Church went (remember the waves of red invading the blue areas on our map in the introduction), it would first wipe out the native Paleopagan clergy and their public worship customs, then, after a few decades or centuries, start hunting and executing heretics. The Roman Church had a vital psychological,

---

*See *The Inquisition* by Fernand Hayward, published by the Church's Society of St. Paul and with a full *Imprimatur* and *Nihil Obstat* (official Church approval) in 1965.

†Most of the bishops and patriarchs from the other forty-five Catholic churches still feel that way today.

political, and theological interest in keeping the attention of Christendom focused on real or imagined enemies. This was similar to how corporate and political leaders in the twentieth century focused the attention of the world on the "communist peril," thus deflecting movements aimed at making them accountable—by declaring those movements to be communist "front groups" and therefore (by the principles of dualism) part of the Forces of Evil.

Through a series of metaphysical gymnastics,* Pope Guilty VIII and the leaders of the Inquisition managed to declare that the *Canon Episcopi* was in essence "irrelevant" or referred to some other cult of a similar description. They couldn't actually say it was "wrong" because it had been considered Church law for hundreds of years.

However, after 1484 it was heresy if one did *not* believe that there were witches who flew through the air and had magical powers given to them by the false deity they worshiped—only now, that deity was said to be Satan instead of Diana. People accused of malevolent witchcraft by guilty or paranoid neighbors suddenly found themselves heretics of a much more frightening sort and liable to execution rather than penance. Thus, the Church created out of thin (if busy) air a brand new kind of "witchcraft," a *religion* of Devil worship, which I originally called Gothic Witchcraft† but will refer to as Diabolic Witchcraft from now on.

The details of Diabolic Witchcraft were easy to invent. Since Roman Catholicism was the only "true" religion, and since Satan was deemed the opposite of their God, Devil worship (or Satanism) must therefore be an exact reversal of Roman Catholicism. (Other Christian sects accused the Diabolic Witches of reversing *their* particular

---

*This is the ancient sport of leaping from unverified assumptions to foregone conclusions without actually traversing the logical space in between and is still quite popular today.

†It should be noted that I coined this term in 1979, before the rise of the Goth subculture of modern vampire fans, who were so-called for their love of gothic horror literature. Now, we have Gothic Wiccans who are just like regular Wiccans (see part three) except for their preferences for scary deities and their more limited fashion choices.

version of the One True Right and Only Way to worship.) From here sprung fully formed the whole concept of the "witches' sabbat" (which we described in the introduction), "Black Masses,"* and the like.

The ancient Roman urban legends about Evil Cultists who profaned sacred things, ate little babies, held wild orgies, and so on previously used against early Christians, and then by them against Paleopagans, Jews, and heretics for centuries, were dusted off and laid at the feet of Diabolic Witches. These lies were repeated constantly, with evidence manufactured to support them. It was rather like what happened in the Satanic Panic of the 1980s (see Jeffery Victor's book of that title) when Americans and Britons decided that there was a global conspiracy of baby-killing devil worshippers sacrificing hundreds of thousands of people in Satanic orgies.

This insanity was (and is) rooted in the dualist paranoia of Christian mythology, which describes an eternal cosmic battle between Good and Evil. Therefore, anyone who was not a good Christian (by local definition) was committing spiritual treason by helping the enemies of Christendom. This was far worse than mere political treason (which was more of a pastime than a crime in those days). Gradually, the power of Satan increased in the Christian mythos, until he was credited with an entire antichurch of his own. The congregation of this antichurch was said to consist of heretics in general and Diabolic Witches in particular.

I will not go into the details of the persecutions (often called the "Burning Times" by modern Witches) against suspected (and therefore "guilty") Diabolic Witches, since most readers may not have strong stomachs. Somewhere between 50,000 and 250,000 women, children, and men were killed. Estimates of the total body count vary widely among scholars, depending on their sources, definitions, biases, and academic fashions, but have been going steadily downward as

---

*Previously, the concept of "Black Masses" had referred to masses (the standard Catholic liturgy) said for the dead—in which Catholic priests usually wore black vestments—only performed for people who were still living, as a kind of curse!

more and better historical research has been done. As Jenny Gibbons
puts it:

> Ever since the Great Hunt itself, we've relied on witch hunters'
> propaganda: witch hunting manuals, sermons against witchcraft,
> and lurid pamphlets on the more sensational trials. Everyone
> knew that this evidence was lousy. It's sort of like trying to study
> Satanism in America using only the *Moral Majority Newsletter* and
> the *National Enquirer.* The few trials cited were the larger, more
> infamous ones. And historians frequently used literary accounts
> of those cases, not the trials themselves. That's comparable to cit-
> ing a television docu-drama ("Based on a true story!") instead of
> actual court proceedings.*

Gibbons also points out that most of the witch killings happened
during the Renaissance, not the Middle Ages, that more killings happened when national governments or the Church were weak in a
given region, and that they were more likely to happen when a noble-
man felt he had been cursed than when a poor person did. So, no,
9 million women weren't killed by the Church as witches, but even a
few dozen, let alone tens or hundreds of thousands of victims, were
far too many.

Accused witches were often raped, maimed, mutilated, and mur-
dered in ways that make the atrocities of modern storm troopers and
death squads look like child's play, although one *could* draw a useful
comparison to the way that *some* American military personnel and
"civilian contractors" have been known to treat prisoners suspected of
being part of the Forces of Evil during the cold war and the current
War on Terrorism. Dehumanizing them is the key. Once you can
convince yourself that your victims "aren't really human," torture is
much easier not only to do but also to justify later.

Most of this, mind you, was what was done during *questioning,* before "guilt" had even been "proven" and sentence passed. The actual
executions could be swift and merciful by contrast: hanging, burning
alive, strangulation, drowning, and so on. In some times and places it

*See appendix 8 again.

was the civilian authorities who supervised the worst of the atrocities and in others, the Church.

The whole pseudolegal point of the torture was to ask the accused person long, involved questions and to force her or him to answer yes or no. The torture continued until the victim "confessed" all she or he was told to say. Then she or he was taken out of the torture room and asked the same questions, with the threat of further torture if she or he did not reaffirm her or his confession. Once a confession was re-affirmed, the courts could state in the official records, "the accused confessed without torture," and send the victim (usually a woman or girl) back to the torture room for the "good Christian men" to do with as they pleased.

These horrors were not confined to Roman Catholicism; after the Protestant Reformation, the new religious leaders agreed with the old that Diabolic Witches deserved to die. So they proceeded to roast accused Diabolic Witches, heretics, Catholics, and each other. The Bible translators working in England managed to insert the English word "witch" into several parts of the scriptures where "a Devil-worshipping sorceress" could not possibly have been meant (the ancient Hebrews had no "Devil" figure for anyone to be worshipping). The infamous "thou shalt not suffer a witch to live" line, for example, actually referred to a poisoner (*kasgagh* in Hebrew), whom it might actually make sense to execute, especially in a tribal society where survival depends on trust. However, the witch-phobic King James, like Christian fundamentalists today, loved how this (mis)translation could justify his hatred and violence toward accused witches.

What, besides the greed and sexual depravity of the Christian clergy and civil authorities, turned witch hunting into a socially accepted activity? Many scholars have offered many theories, ranging from the Church's fear of the dawning scientific worldview, to a sexist reaction against strong women, to a homophobic reaction against real or alleged lesbians and gay men, to a way to get rid of social dissidents, to a way to distract attention away from the real evildoers. All these theories have something to offer, so we should not let ourselves be trapped by monothesisism, by insisting on a single explanation.

One popular theory today, first published in *Witches, Midwives, and Nurses* by Barbara Erinreich, is that it was a conspiracy by medical doctors against midwives and amateur healers. This doesn't hold much water, however, as midwives and cunning folk were seldom accused of being witches—on the contrary, they were often witnesses against alleged witches, both criminal and diabolic.

Part of the answer, I feel, lies in the fear that magic and psychic phenomena can cause in ignorant people. Even the cunning folk had inspired fear as well as respect. With ten centuries of Church propaganda drumming it into the populace's heads that all magic came from either Jehovah or Satan, more fear of magic workers developed. When the Black Plague wiped out a third of Europe's population almost overnight, preachers were quick to suggest that it was punishment from the Christian God for laxity in Christendom. Jews, "Gypsies," strangers, and other unusual people were scapegoated on an unprecedented scale. They had always been subject to accusations of witchcraft, and the Jews to ones of Devil worship, so things became even worse for these minorities.

One note of true irony is that the creation of Diabolic Witchcraft by the Church did manage to produce actual diabolic groups—not among the peasantry, but at the Court of Louis XIV, the king of France. Members of the highest ranks of the nobility, trying to relieve their royal boredom, reportedly engaged in hideous crimes and asinine theatrics, holding Black Masses and slaughtering infants just as the Church had told them was the way it was properly done. In 1662, their cover was blown, a scandal ensued, and many of the middle- class and poor people involved were punished (though few of the nobles were, of course). In that same year, by a curious coincidence, Louis issued an edict that, in effect, restrained witchcraft trials throughout France.

For more details on this whole, sick mess, consult Robbins's *The Encyclopedia of Witchcraft and Demonology* (but don't trust his numbers), Briggs's *Witches and Neighbors*, Stuart Clark's *Thinking with Demons* and Jeffrey B. Russell's *A History of Witchcraft: Sorcerers, Heretics, and Pagans*.

# CHAPTER 5

# Witches as Pagan Cultists?

## THE THEORIES OF MARGARET MURRAY

Let us sing for Margaret Murray, who first planted a
small seed
When she said that Witchcraft was a Pagan creed.
Now I wonder if she knew the kind of fuss that she
would stir up
When she wrote about her *Witchcult in Western Europe*?

as there actually a secret, underground movement to act
as the peg on which the Church and state could hang
their branding irons? Could the cunning folk have actually been the leaders of a European-wide Pagan revival
or survival, a Paganism that the Church merely distorted into a
Satanic cult? Let's try to be as generous as possible to these ideas,
without being gullible.

Since the cunning folk would commonly be among the elder
members of any village social structure—it takes a long time to become adept at healing, herbalism, or divination—they *could* have
been at the front of any sporadic efforts to preserve Pagan customs.
They *could* have helped to organize dances, parades, and other folk
customs with which tiny remnants of the old religions could have
been kept alive. However, we have no historical record of anyone who
was called a "witch" (either the original criminal sort or the diabolic)
ever doing so.

Furthermore, as Ronald Hutton shows in *The Stations of the Sun* and *The Rise and Fall of Merry England*, many of the customs we have long been taught were Paleopagan survivals were really medieval or Renaissance inventions. Therefore, the little we can plausibly say about the cunning folk is a far cry from the now well-known theories of an organized cult of Pagan "witches" spanning the entire continent.

Margaret Murray (1863–1963) is the writer most associated with these theories. In this chapter, I want to look at her ideas and how plausible or implausible they appear to modern scholars, before returning in the following chapters to a more historical discussion of those academics who preceded and followed her on this topic.

In the early twentieth century, after a moderately successful career as an Egyptologist, Murray decided to study a topic she apparently knew nothing about: Renaissance Christian history and the great witch hunts. In 1921, Murray published her ideas in *The Witch-Cult in Western Europe*. Academic journals at the time reviewed it and declared it nonsense. Most Britons, however, didn't read academic journals, and Murray's nonacademic readers found her theories attractive.

Murray's next book, *The God of the Witches*, came out in 1933. By this time, archeologists and anthropologists had cast doubt on the theory of a universal "Golden" matriarchal age (see chapter 7), in large part by arguing that there didn't seem to be any primitive tribes (past or then present) that were matriarchal—except for the legendary Amazons—and very few that were even egalitarian. Folklorists and other scholars had begun to show the enormous variation of folk beliefs throughout Europe and had torn the theories in Murray's first book to shreds. Nonetheless, Murray went even further out on her limb, claiming that witches throughout the Continent had worshiped the same Goddess and Horned God, following Sir James Frazer's theories (also chapter 7) exactly, and had set up a political underground as well as a religious one, dedicated to overthrowing the Church and state alike, as in *Aradia* (again, see chapter 7).

In 1954, Murray published *The Divine King in England*, in which she claimed, essentially, that every king of England had died ritually, as in Frazer's *Golden Bough* (including the one who died with a redhot poker up his rear). By this time there were few scholars in the world who would believe any of her arguments. But, as we shall see, there were plenty of would-be witches (then as now) happy to accept all or most of them.

Why were the major conclusions she came to in her books so astonishing, both to her contemporary and modern scholars? Let's look at them more closely.

Murray argued that there *had* been a gigantic, anti-Christian cult in medieval and Renaissance Europe—only it had been Pagan instead of diabolic. Furthermore, the leaders of this cult *might* have been the people called witches, which Murray considered to have been the descendants of the postulated priestesses of "the Old Religion." This religion, she speculated, was a belief system based on the worship of Diana (and Her male counterpart Dianus—a very minor Roman deity) and was so well organized that every witch in Europe had essentially the same theology, ethics, cosmology, and rituals.

A "Dianic Witch"* could supposedly travel from Denmark to Italy or from England to Poland and be accepted into the local services. This, she said, was why the persecutions happened—there really was a gigantic threat to Christianity, only it was run by *Pagan* witches, some of whom were clergy and most of whom were worshippers.

This is an important theory that needs discussion, for many Neopagan Witches and Feminist Witches (see chapters 9 and 10) accept it as "proven" and it has been published as absolute truth in many books, including a few encyclopedias (Murray wrote the *Britannica* entries on witchcraft for several editions).

To begin with, Murray took the "confessions" wrung from the supposed diabolic witches and compared their artificially constructed similarities (descriptions of the sabbats, stories about signing a contract with the Devil, etc.), which had been caused by the inquisitors'

---

*Murray was the first to use this term, now used mostly for feminist separatist Witches (see chapter 10).

and civil courts' use of standard torture manuals, with collections of folk beliefs and customs from England, Brittany, and Italy (done by some of the scholars we'll meet in chapter 7).

Unfortunately for the romantics among us, evidence in favor of witches (either as suspected magical criminals or as cunning folk) being the leaders of a religion of *any* sort is simply nonexistent. Neither is there evidence of any "universal" cults (of specific, named deities) among European Paleopagans, while contrary evidence is plentiful (serious readers may wish to consult the Paleopagan section of appendix 5). Similarity between the mythologies and religious customs of the Indo-European peoples is not the same as identity of belief and practice (that "similarity equals identity" idea is a trap that dualists often fall into). Within specific language families, there might be similar deities with similar-sounding names such as Bride, Bridget, and Brigantia (or Lugh and Llew) among the speakers of Celtic languages, but that doesn't become universal either, since the European tribes speaking Germanic or Italic tongues don't have deities by these names. Knowledge held by Paleopagan healers, midwives, and cunning folk may have been passed along to (or reinvented by) their Mesopagan descendants, but that is not the same thing as a structured religion being passed along from generation to generation. Furthermore, we *know* who the clergy of the old religions were—they were the druids, godis, flamens, and so on. However, for the sake of argument, let us pretend for a few moments there really was a unified Old Religion of some sort throughout all of Europe, which survived intact into the Christian era. Could the customs and beliefs of such a cult have survived 500 to 1,500 years (depending on where in Europe we're looking) of suppression by a dominating religion utterly opposed to it?

There are certain factors required for the safe transmittal of an organized religious tradition from generation to generation. It must be written down and physically preserved, or else it must become part of an oral literature supported by public approval of the bards, actors, and storytellers. Either way, it will usually be altered by the requirements of the literary, theatrical, or poetic forms used, as well as by the religious expectations of the intended audience. A good example of such traditions being passed down can be found in the Indian families who memorized chapters of the *Vedas* and passed these down from generation to generation so effectively that even in the twentieth century their descendants could recite their chapters and match the oldest written versions word for word.

Unfortunately, there are no equivalents yet discovered to the *Vedas*, the *Eddas*, or the *Mabinogion* (collected tales of Indic, Norse, and Welsh mythology, respectively) that might present the entire mythology of the hypothesized "Universal Witch Cult" as practiced by our supposed predecessors. Granted, a large number of people have claimed that the previously mentioned texts are just chock full of references to the Old Religion and are really about the Witch Cult. The fact remains, however, that any sacred scriptures of the postulated Witch Cult's beliefs and practices (with the exception of quotes from old poems and folk songs) were never found in written form until the last sixty years,* while their supposed beliefs simply do not match what we know of the various Indo-European Paleopagan religions.†

Christianity did not provide much in the way of support for competing religions. The Church accepted some local planting and herding customs and holidays, turned some of the local deities and nature spirits into saints and demons, and went merrily on its way subverting and co-opting the faiths of the conquered tribes. Granted, it could be argued that as an underground movement, the Witch Cult might have provided a subculture that gave semipublic support to an oral literature of religious witchcraft.

But Europe of the Middle Ages and the Renaissance was not the England or America of today, where religious subcultures may be tolerated, even if despised. A subculture has to be substantial to provide

*Or a little over a century ago, if we count *Aradia*, published in 1899 by Charles Leland (see chapter 7).
†See chapter 12's discussion of Wiccan beliefs.

the necessary amount of financial and social support to keep a full religion going underground. Bards have to eat, after all, and have appreciative audiences, and so do dramatists, dancers, and polytheologians. Long before any survival or revival could have reached the necessary size, it would have been subverted or destroyed by the Church.

It's useful here to look at the *maranos*, a secret underground of Jews in Catholic Spain. In 1492, the king of Spain ordered all Jews to leave Spain, convert to Catholicism, or be executed. Many left, many died, but many others chose to convert, some of them under false pretenses. These "underground" Jews practiced their faith in secrecy while acting in public as good Catholics. When caught, they were referred to as *maranos*, Spanish for "pigs"—used because it was a word especially insulting to Jews, who considered pigs unclean animals.

After World War II, many of the maranos went public, demanding to be allowed to immigrate to Israel under the "Right of Return," which says Jews anywhere in the world have a right to move to Israel and become citizens. To determine the validity of their claim, the government of Israel sent a team of linguists, anthropologists, and rabbis to Spain to interview them. The maranos, they discovered, knew that they were supposed to study the Old Testament and ignore the New, light candles and say special prayers on Friday nights and Saturdays, and use mezuzahs and other Jewish talismans their ancestors had hidden away. That, and a handful of Hebrew words, was all the maranos knew about being Jewish (for details, read *The Mezuzah in the Madonna's Foot* by Trudi Alexy).

Thus, we have a group of highly literate people with a rich and deep tradition of organized religious beliefs and practices, who lost 99 percent of it after only 500 years underground. Just how likely is it then that Paleopagans, most of them illiterate, would have been able to keep their religion alive for 500 to 1,500 years (depending on where in Europe you start counting) without public support for families of myth-memorizing clergy?

Yes, the medieval peasants built ritual fires at certain times of the year; and yes, they followed the agricultural customs of their ancestors (and invented new ones). None of these activities prove, however, that they had any idea, magically or religiously, of what they were doing. This is why later outside observers make remarks such as, "The peasants really did this because . . ." or "They were actually worshiping an old Pagan god named Murphy, who . . ."

*You do not need a religious or magical reason to perform customary or enjoyable acts.* The mere fact that, "This is the way my grandfather did it," or that, "Actually, I've always rather enjoyed orgies," is more than sufficient to ensure that some form of that act will be perpetuated. After all, in magic and religion as in many other fields, you do not have to consciously understand what you are doing to get results (though it usually helps). Just because a group of peasants is performing a ritual of possible magical efficacy, or one that is at least constructed according to the basic laws of magic, does not prove that they have had someone train them in the art of magic. Nor does a belief that a ritual is old and authentic make it so.

To the average medieval peasant, the Church provided nearly every religious comfort that the old belief systems did, except for one area of life: sex. The Church provided nothing except monogamous marriage to fill that niche. So it was all the more likely that older sexual customs (such as making love out in the fields just before or after planting to make the seed fertile) would be preserved, with or without a magical or theological context that would provide a deeper meaning. But it is entirely possible that the peasants just wanted to have some fun, not worship the Old Gods. After all, modern teenagers did not invent wild parties.

Murray thought that the supposed witches' sabbats (those diabolical gatherings described in the introduction) were peasant orgies out in the woods. I'm willing to grant that the peasants *might* have gone into the woods to hold orgies, but as Sybil Leek once told me, people who believe that have probably never spent a night in the woods in Great Britain—it's cold and damp out there at night! Real orgies would have been far more likely to happen in barns and haystacks close to home.

The witch persecutions peaked between roughly 1450 and 1650, finally petering out first in western Europe, then in central and southern Europe throughout the 1700s. In all that time, with all those murders, very little proof was ever produced—that would stand up in a modern court of law, anyway—to show the existence of an organized Pagan (or Diabolic) cult among the peasantry. Two possible Mesopagan exceptions were the cult of Aradia (see chapter 7) and that of the quasi-shamanic *Benandanti* ("good walkers") in sixteenth and seventeenth century Italy (discussed in Carlo Ginzburg's *The Night Battles*), which apparently conceived of itself as an *anti*-witch cult and its members as good Christians.*

I will grant that it was fashionable for scholars a hundred years ago, such as Frazer and Charles Leland (see chapter 7), to interpret many European folk customs such as hobby-horse parades or Morris dancing as Paleopagan survivals under thin Christian veneers. However, even if some of them were genuine customs from the Paleopagan times (which Hutton tells us is unlikely), there is little or nothing to suggest that the people practicing these customs knew they were doing something Pagan, that they were in touch with each other, or that they shared more than the vaguest of common beliefs.

Here is the hard truth about honest research and debate: While it is impossible to prove absolute negatives, we can look at the weight of the evidence to see whether a claim appears likely, possible, or far-fetched. When there is little or no evidence to support the existence of something that was supposedly widely spread through both time and space, as both the Church and Margaret Murray claimed, the odds are it didn't exist.

If I say that there were green cows raised all over Europe for two thousand years, yet there are no historical, religious, or artistic references to green cows from any European country during that time

*See *The Night Battles: Witchcraft and Agrarian Cults in the Sixteenth and Seventeenth Century*, by Carlo Ginzburg, 1983/1992 (English translation); also his *Ecstasies: Deciphering the Witches' Sabbath* (2004).

period, you would be fully justified in concluding that there probably weren't any. The fact that we might both want desperately to believe in green cows doesn't save the concept from its improbability.

Even though Murray's speculations were to become central themes in what would come to be known as the "Myth of Wicca" in the mid-twentieth century, I'm afraid the theories of both the Inquisition and Margaret Murray about the Great Underground Witchcraft Conspiracy must be dismissed as highly unlikely at best and utter nonsense at worst.

# CHAPTER 6

# Family Tradition, Immigrant Tradition, and Ethnic Witches

Let us praise our many Grandmas, anonymous and meek,
With their ancient Craft traditions that we just made up last
week.
When it comes down to grandmothers, and all is done and
said,
One who simply can't speak English works as well as one
who's dead.

ould there have been links between underground Pagans who were *not* peasants? Based on the well-known historical principle that rich people don't get persecuted as much as poor people do, it has been suggested that throughout Europe and the British Isles it would have been possible for wealthy families and minor nobility to quietly continue Paleo-pagan practices as private "family business." Since European nobility usually married other nobility (leading to a number of problems with inherited diseases), such underground Pagans might have kept their customs going for a long time, even into the twentieth century.

Tempting though this theory might be to those who long for Pagan survivals, it ignores the important fact that many inquisitors and civil judges chose rich or well-off victims precisely *because* they had wealth, which would then be split between the Church and the local secular authorities.

However, if we focus on minor nobility, we might have more luck in constructing this particular house of (tarot?) cards. Considering that even today these local leaders, who live in small cities and outside of large towns, are notoriously conservative about family customs, it is *possible* that some such survivors of the witch hunts might have prospered, while keeping their family secrets. Whether such families thought of themselves as being "witches" of any sort, or "Pagans," or (more likely) just plain "family" cannot now be determined.

I have met people who claim to be descended from such families, and they have usually referred to themselves as witches. To describe these people—and to my ever-lasting regret—I coined the term Family Tradition Witches (Fam-Trads), though one could also consider some of them merely Neoclassic Witches (see chapter 8). I regret coining the term because scores of dishonest people subsequently used it to describe themselves in the Neopagan community and on-line to impress the gullible and to avoid having to provide proofs of their claims.

Historically, however, the minor nobility, unlike the wealthier and more traveled major nobility, were often highly suspicious of out-siders—even those from their own country, let alone foreigners. This is infertile ground from which a complex communication network, strung out across scores of European cultures, could have sprung, as hypothesized by Margaret Murray and her followers.

Thus, while it's *possible* that Fam-Trads exist today and have been for many generations practicing customs some of them *now* describe as "witchcraft" (either Wiccan or "witchcraft-with-a-small-w"), there is no real evidence that the influence of any given family (unless they were royalty or upper nobility) would have spread more than a hundred miles or so, at least not before the twentieth century. There is also no convincing evidence that any customs handed down by these hypothetical families would have been uncontaminated Paleopagan customs (rather than Mesopagan survivals) and/or would have been in agreement with the beliefs many Neopagan and Feminist Witches assume the postulated Witch Cult had. On the contrary, there is a great deal of evidence against both of these possibilities, especially the former. I suppose that it is possible that members of some families of wealthy underground occultists might have read books about Greco-Roman witchcraft and tried to incorporate those ideas into a form of Mesopagan witchcraft religion, which they could have passed on to their descendants, but again we have no evidence that this ever happened until the twentieth century.

After the Burning Times finally ended in the seventeenth century, no one seemed very interested in witches anymore. Modern Europe was dawning and the powers of the churches dwindling, at least among the intellectuals of the day. Freemasonry, Rosicrucianism, Theosophy, and Spiritualism were sweeping over Europe and America, along with the mechanistic and dualistic worldview of Science (which became a new religion for many). All these new belief systems had drastic effects on rich and poor alike.

Millions of peasants emigrated from Europe to the Americas, most of them the descendants of farmers and serfs. Others came as convicted criminals or indentured servants, working for wealthy land-owners. It is possible, in some cases, that the rich émigrés *could* have been members of Fam-Trads of underground occultists, sent to earn their fortune, to establish new holdings, or to escape quasi-legal persecution at home. It's also possible that the poor immigrants could have continued with their Mesopagan ways out in the colonial boondocks.

If so, most likely it would have been those settlers originally from the wilder parts of northern and eastern Europe, such as Lithuania or the mountains of Germany, where Paleopaganism lingered longest, who would have had the most remaining bits of Pagan customs. These people might then have mixed their beliefs and magical practices with those of the Native American and African-descended peoples they would meet in the New World. Years ago, I designated these *highly* postulated witches Immigrant Tradition Witches (Imm-Trads; admittedly not my most felicitous abbreviation).

The Pennsylvania Dutch (*Deutch,* or German) communities in-cluded *hexmeisters* among them (some of whom I *might* be descended from), but their "powwow" spells consist mostly of Christian prayers said over the usual magical links, not anything remotely Paleopagan. *Hexmeister* means "witch master," not in the sense of a master of witchcraft but of one who could master, that is, control witches. This would put such people squarely as cunning folk rather than as witches, but it would also imply that the concept of criminal witch-craft was still alive and well as recently as the nineteenth century.

The "hoodoo doctors" of old New Orleans were essentially cun-ning folk of mixed racial backgrounds, the majority of whose cus-tomers were among the poor and oppressed, but they were often referred to as "witches" by white folks who didn't know any better. Indeed, the native healers and cunning folk of many nonwhite cul-tures, and even their priests and priestesses, were often erroneously called witches. Again, I coined a term for this, "Ethnic Witches," which, like Imm-Trad Witches, I now consider unnecessary.

Over the last few centuries of scientific development, cunning folk in Europe and North America seem to have dwindled in prestige, but *if* there were, in fact, Fam-Trad Witches existing in those places, they would not have been so badly affected. Being, as postulated, better educated and more intellectual, they might have had a sophisticated enough set of metaphysics—and a better understanding of magic and psychic powers—so that new ideas would have been less traumatic. However, since Scientism was rapidly becoming the supreme religion in the West, it is reasonable to suppose that most members of Fam-Trads would have made efforts to conceal their "superstitious" beliefs and magical systems.

Some might have gotten involved in Freemasonry and Rosicru-cianism in the eighteenth century, or Spiritualism and Theosophy in the nineteenth. All these movements were more respectable than witchcraft, and would still have allowed the members of Fam-Trads to practice occult arts, albeit with increasingly Christian and non-European spiritual and magical content.

It is a reasonable *speculation* that, as the years went by, members of the postulated Fam-Trads would have absorbed and incorporated more and more from these other sources, handing new information as well as old down to the next generations. They *might* have carelessly let their descendants think that a Rosicrucian spell or alchemical meditation was a legitimate part of an ancient Pagan heritage. Thus, by today we would have Fam-Trad Witches who would be closer to being Theosophists or Spiritualists than to being cunning folk—and as such, darned unlikely to call themselves "witches" of any sort!

As modern medicine and pharmacology developed, fewer people would turn to any remaining cunning folk for aid. Except in isolated villages, it appears that folk magic in western and southern Europe slowly died out. Not much is known (in English resources anyway) about what happened to similar people in eastern and northern Europe.

I believe that the dying-out process was much slower there for two reasons: first, because material technology did not spread as quickly in those regions, especially outside the cities, so the preindustrial skills of cunning folk would have remained useful longer. Second, these areas were Christianized later than the southern and western regions, so the people had more of their Pagan beliefs and practices left at the time religious authority collapsed in the face of scientific authority.

Indeed, in Lithuania and other Baltic states, Paleopagan and/or Mesopagan survivals were reported well into the twentieth century. People were dressing up in white robes and going into the forests, swamps, and mountains to worship the Old Lithuanian Gods. It's possible, however, that these were the Mesopagan results of artificially created nationalist revivals of folk customs, similar to what produced the fraternal Mesopagan Druid movements in France and England in the eighteenth century.*

In the mid-to-late twentieth century, however, most (if not all) of the people who came forward claiming to have secret family traditions of *religious* Witchcraft were, in point of fact, lying (or had been

*See *Bonewits's Essential Guide to Druidism* for details.

lied to by their teachers). What they had were either a mix of a dozen Judeo-Christian magical systems with a few folk customs stuck in here and there, or else obvious derivations of Wicca as created by Gerald Gardner and friends (see chapter 8), often with some ethnic window-dressing and claims that "Gardner stole it from us." Some of these people even wrote best-selling* books about their supposed ancient underground Pagan traditions, all of which wound up sounding just like Wicca, whether called that or not.

A number of very sincere students studied with these fake Fam-Trads and went on to teach the same lies to their students as ancient truths. Their students did the same, so today we have many Neo-pagan Witches (see part three) who sincerely believe that what they do in ritual is genuinely ancient. Fortunately, historical authenticity is usually irrelevant to magical and religious power. It's been said that my refusal to be gullible about the claims of Fam-Trads shows that I have "contempt for the sacred oral traditions of the Craft." Claiming that all the evidence is oral rather than written does explain away the absence of textual proof, but none of the people arguing this have offered to recite several hours' worth of supposedly ancient lore—in an ancient language—from memory, as real holders of oral traditions are capable of doing. Nor does labeling their materials "sacred" mean that they are beyond questioning. Of course, since the same people who claim to have a sacred oral tradition of Pagan religious Witchcraft also insist that their proofs must remain forever secret, no one can ever find out whether they are real or not without subjecting themselves to their training systems and oaths, so the supposed evidence is useless from a scholarly point of view and highly suspicious from an ethical one.

Another tactic that has been tried over the last decade or so has been to claim that the sources Gerald Gardner took his ideas from had gotten *their* ideas from the real Old Religion of Pagan Witchcraft, which continued to exist into modern times. So people claiming

---

*In modern Pagan terms, that means over a 1,000 copies.

to belong to Family Traditions of Witchcraft—that just happen to highly resemble what Gardner put together—can say their materials are from those older sources, passed down through the generations. Such people will usually describe ancient and modern folk magic from their favorite ethnic group, mention many bits and pieces of authentic Paleopaganism (such as deity names, holy days, and so forth) that are known to have existed before Christianity and which their Tradition now supposedly uses, refer to *Aradia* and other books by Charles Leland (see chapter 7) as evidence that Mesopagan cults survived into modern times, and then blithely skip over any logical connections between these various items and their current claims. This quickly slides into assertionism, which is the idea that merely making the same claim over and over makes it true. "Of course there's no proof that the people who initiated me and all their predecessors have an unbroken link to the ancient past. They would have been killed if they left evidence lying around. How *dare* you imply that this isn't true!" So absence of evidence is magically transformed into evidence of presence for supposed ancient Family Traditions of Witchcraft, because the speakers know that most people are too polite to really demand evidence of religious claims.

Does it all really matter? Perhaps not. It could be simply a matter of the Myth of Wicca evolving to meet the needs of a new generation of religious founders. Yet I can't help but remember that when religions are founded on lies, or even just claims that are impossible to verify, sooner or later those religions get dangerous to their members, if not their neighbors.

# CHAPTER 7

# It Made Sense at the Time

## The Early Social Scientists'
## Contributions to the Discussion

Let us sing for Sir James Frazer, a scholar and a gent.
To rescue Pagan customs by the Old Gods he was sent.
Ten thousand pages filled with who, what, where, when,
    why, and how;
For the treasures that he gave us he should take a *Golden
Bough*.

rom 1860 to 1880, the scholar J. J. Bachofen (1815–1887) conjectured, from predominately speculative etymological evidence and an argument that "primitive" peoples were ignorant about paternity, that there had been an "Age of Mother Right" early in human prehistory. By this he meant not a matriarchy in which women ruled men tyranically, but a time in which women were more socially, culturally, and politically equal to men than they were in the later monotheistic era—which would, of course, be true of most of human existence. Indeed, we know today that most European Paleopagan women did have more egalitarian relations with their men than their unhappy Christian descendants had. Bachofen's thinking, however, was based on dualistic logic and Social Darwinism, the idea that human social systems evolved like species did, with "better" ones replacing "poorer" ones—

a notion then quite fashionable among the upper-class white men ruling the Western world.

Two obscure writers named Karl Marx (1818–1883) and Friedrich Engels* (1820–1895), the founders of Marxism, adopted and expanded Bachofen's Age of Mother Right idea. Marx thought it logical that an "inferior" society run by women (note how they dualistically rejected the idea that the genders might have been equal) would have naturally preceded the innately "superior" ones run by men. Eventually, this concept of a matriarchal age became an integral part of Marxist theory. Though hardly anyone except dogmatic Marxist theoreticians talk about it anymore, it was an extremely popular idea among the intellectuals of the day and was later adopted by feminist theoreticians attracted to the idea that women had once ruled the world. During the 1980s, feminist writers (most of whom had no actual historical training) turned this idea into one of a "Matriarchal Golden Age."

From 1880 to 1900, much important work was done in the archeology of the Mediterranean region and in comparative mythology and folklore (the study of other people's religious beliefs). Sir James Frazer (1854–1941) published the first volume of his multivolume *Golden Bough* series in 1890, proposing his theories about the presence of the "Divine King" and goddess worship in most European cultures, based on his research into current folklore among Europeans and the alleged beliefs of "primitive" peoples around the world. In 1897, Karl Pearson (1857–1936) published a speech he had given six years earlier, "Woman as Witch," as an essay in *The Chances of Death and Other Studies in Evolution.*[†] Pearson had investigated European folklore and the witch hunts and had concluded that the "witches" had been holdovers from Bachofen's Age of Mother Right.

Bachofen, Marx, Engles Frazer, and Pearson provided the theories that would be used by major figures in the soon to come witchcraft

---

*See *Origins of the Family, Private Property, and the State, in Light of the Researches of Lewis H. Morgan* by Friedrich Engles, 1891.

[†] *The Chances of Death and Other Studies in Evolution* by Karl Pearson, OP.

revival (see chapter 8). They also influenced those scholars who interpreted the "Venus" figurines (found by archeologists in various parts of Europe and originally called such in ridicule because they were fat and "ugly") as evidence for a universal goddess cult entrenched within a postulated Near Eastern and European matriarchal society.

In 1899, the relatively respected folklorist Charles Leland (1824–1903) published *Aradia: or, the Gospel of the Witches of Tuscany.* The manuscript was provided to him, after much pestering, by his Italian informant (and possible mistress), a woman named Maddelena. He then combined this with materials from his earlier books on folk magic. It was a study of the alleged beliefs of the members of a peasant culture in northern Italy about what they supposedly called the "Old Religion." The book contained stories, legends, rites, and traditions concerning a goddess named Aradia, who was the messianic Queen of the Witches, having inherited her powers from her mother, Diana, and her father, Lucifer. It shows a heavy Christian influence and the customs contained do not seem to go directly back further than the seventeenth century or so. But *Aradia* does show that at least *some* peasants might have retained (or regained) self-images as Pagans even unto the turn of the twentieth century—unless Maddelena forged it.

Maddelena was apparently a cunning woman who had been collecting folklore materials for Leland for several years, most of which depicted witches as evil. Leland, however, had heard rumors about a secret book that described a *religion* of witches and, after much urging, Maddelena finally produced a manuscript for him. It has been suggested (and hotly debated) that she may have written it herself to please Leland; but Leland thought it reasonably authentic in that it repeated at greater length things she had already told him verbally (although that assumed she hadn't been lying to him all along). Leland edited this book, as he had two previous ones based on materials supplied in part by Maddelena (*Etruscan Roman Remains* and *Legends of Florence*), with his own assumptions about surviving Paleopagan beliefs and practices. He also mixed his references to cunning folk and witches, despite the former occupation's hostility to the latter.

If the document was authentic, it is amusing to think that in 1899, but a stone's throw away from Rome, there was a Mesopagan cult (still?) active. Could this have been a direct survival of those "abandoned women" the Church said believed that they flew through the night with Diana? *Perhaps.* Could Maddelena have been one of their priestesses? *Maybe.* Could it have been a direct descendant of some earlier cult of Paleopagan times? *Possibly.*

However, there had been enough of an obsession with Greek and Roman mythology by Renaissance artists and scholars that Paleo-pagan beliefs could have been resurrected (in a highly mutated form) by the gradual sifting down of data to the peasants. *Perhaps* some started worshiping Diana just to spite the Christian clergy. Centuries later, their Mesopagan descendants *might* believe that they had worshiped Her continuously. This, of course, is pure speculation. It is entirely possible that among the wild hills of Tuscany (and elsewhere in Italy and Sicily) Mesopagan beliefs and practices *might* have survived, including a cult of Diana and Her daughter. Yet if that is the case, what happened to the cults of all the other Roman and Etruscan gods and goddesses? After all, the "Old Religion" in Italy had *many* deities!

Let us leave *Aradia* for the moment and return to our historical travelogue. As many people today tend to forget, in Africa, Asia, and the Americas, different cultures had people they considered what we here have been calling criminal witches, and anthropologists wrote a great deal about these witches and the witch doctors/medicine people who "detected" them, much as the cunning folk did in Europe. Interestingly, in many of the "primitive" cultures, people believed that some folks could be involuntary criminal witches, that is, that they could be monsters born with the ability to curse others just by looking at them—something very similar to what southern Europeans call the "evil eye." Indeed, this became part of how the new science of anthropology defined "witchcraft."

From 1900 to 1920, the fields of comparative religious studies, mythology, folklore, anthropology, archeology, sociology, and psychology began to develop as "real" sciences in Europe and America. A tremendous glut of conflicting data and theory was amassed that would be mined for decades, heavily influenced by academic and cultural fashions reaching back to the eighteenth century. Tons of books were published on the beliefs (real or imagined) of Paleopagan cultures, folk societies, and nonliterate tribes around the world. The power of tribal magical systems became evident to researchers, though many (for racist, creedist, and ethnocentric reasons) preferred not to admit this. Monothesisism was the order of the day as everyone looked for the grand theory that would explain everything.

During these same years, the public became more aware of psychical research. Both Spiritualism and Theosophy became popular, and ceremonial magic was being revived in England and Europe. In the British Isles, the Hermetic Order of the Golden Dawn (HOGD; the most famous occult order of its time) had attracted influential artists, poets, and other mystically inclined intellectuals from its beginning in 1888 to its splintering in the early twentieth century.

World War I put an end to the isolation of many villages in Europe, forcibly bringing the survivors into the twentieth century. Many peasant cultures, with whatever Mesopagan customs they might have had, were irrevocably disrupted, while exposure to modern medicine and science shrank the market for cunning folk to sell their services.

Sometime between 1920 and 1925 in England (according to personal conversations with Sybil Leek and Gavin Frost—whom we will meet later), a few folklorists seem to have gotten together with some members of the HOGD, as well as Mesopagan Druids, Rosicrucians, Theosophists, cunning folk, and a few supposed Fam-Trad Witches to produce the first modern "covens" in England, based on Murray's ideas. It seems clear that they were grabbing eclectically from any source they could find to try and reconstruct the shards of their imagined—and highly romantic—Pagan past.

CHAPTER 8

# The Parents, Aunts, Uncles, and Feuding Cousins of Wicca

Let us sing for Gerald Gardner, he's the father of us all.
When the Goddess needed help, he quickly answered Her call.
He loved the Goddess dearly, through many a fair maid,
And to tell you all his secrets I would need *High Magick's Aid.*

 any people were responsible for the creation of the religion that was to become known as Wicca in the middle of the twentieth century. Though some of them may remain forever unknown, we will meet many of them in this chapter (and remeet a few familiar faces). One man stands head and shoulders above the rest: the amateur scholar, occultist, and romantic visionary who became a passionate lover of the Goddess, Gerald Brousseau Gardner (1884–1964)—who can truly be called the Father of Wicca.*

In 1938, this retired British civil servant met the members of the Rosicrucian Fellowship of Crotona and their Rosicrucian Theatre.

*Even if some of us do sometimes call him Uncle Gerald (along with Old Gerald, GBG, and other nicknames).

The fellowship had started as a lodge in the mixed-gender form of Freemasonry (called Co-Masonry) founded in the 1920s by Annie Besant (1847–1933), well known as an early social reformer and Theosophical leader, who became interested in Rosicrucianism (a Mesopagan occult system focused on a highly Christianized form of sexual mysticism). But inside the fellowship there supposedly existed an inner circle, this one calling itself the New Forest Coven and claiming to be a group of underground Witches who had kept the "Old Religion" of Witchcraft alive.

It seems that the lodge, the theatre, and the coven—which may have been overlapping, rather than subsets of one another—were, as Fred Lamond, a surviving member of Gardner's last coven (see below), puts it:

> Three experimental groups practicing Theosophy, Rosicrucian magic, and reconstructed witchcraft according to the theories of Margaret Murray. It was the latter group that Gerald joined, and in which he found "everything he had longed for all his life," according to his biography *Gerald Gardner: Witch* [written by Sufi scholar Idries Shah, under the name of the journalist Jack Bracelin].

Gardner was later to say that all the members of the coven were very old and apparently the last of their kind and that since their beliefs and practices were "fragmented and incomplete," he took upon himself the task of researching and writing new rituals, customs, and beliefs. He never does say how much the supposed older members approved of his efforts, but he devoted the rest of his life to the project, working in a highly eclectic fashion. In 1939, Gardner published his first (bad) novel, *A Goddess Arrives*, based in part on a vision he had of the Goddess some years earlier in Cyprus. She was to become ever more central to his life's work. Lamond told me:

> Gerald admitted that the group's [small] membership consisted largely of middle class intellectuals with a large element of ex-

colonial administrators like him. And he said its rituals were "sketchy." Where Gardner starts being creative with the truth is when he claimed the New Forest Coven included among its members a couple of hereditary cunning men and that these provided the continuous initiatory link to Stone Age witchcraft. While I have not seen the New Forest Coven's membership list—for obvious reasons, this was highly oath bound—I must say that any cunning men among their members kept their knowledge very much to themselves. The stock in trade of British cunning men was horse-whispering (a benign horse training method recently publicized by Monty Roberts*) and weather magic, while their partners the wise women were (or are as some of them are still around) highly knowledgeable of medicinal plants. None of this was ever passed on by Gerald: his spell-casting was strictly and only mental thought projection boosted by the raising of physical/emotional power.

. . . I visited Cecil Williamson [a well-known British occultist] in 1994 and asked him about his recollections of witchcraft groups in the New Forest area. He told me that after Margaret Murray published her *Witch Cult in Western Europe* in 1924, many magical groups started looking for hereditary cunning men and/or wise women to join their groups and instruct them about what witches actually did. According to Cecil, these cunning men listened carefully to what the magical groups' preconceptions were and then fed these back to them, but didn't volunteer any information that the magical groups didn't already have. So it is quite possible that the Crotona Fellowship went hunting high and low for genuine horny-handed sons of the soil to join their experimental witchcraft group and got two, but this would explain why these cunning men never passed on their herbal and weather control knowledge. Gerald probably genuinely believed that their presence gave his group a lineage back to the Stone Age because that is what he wanted to believe himself.

Such reticence on the part of cunning men would have been fully in keeping with the habits of magicians everywhere. If what you

---

*See *The Man Who Listens to Horses* by Monty Roberts (1997).

know (that others don't) is your stock in trade, you don't go around casually telling it to other people who might be thinking of going into competition with you! This would also explain why the stuff Gardner does reveal about the supposed coven's knowledge doesn't include the skills of the cunning folk who were probably the closest living thing to the Classic Witch archetype.

Gardner worked on his project throughout World War II, taking material from any source that didn't run away too fast. One source that didn't run at all was the (in)famous occultist, poet, "pervert," and Mesopagan prophet* Aleister Crowley (1875–1947), whom Gardner met only a few months before the latter's death.

Gardner joined Crowley's ceremonial magic organization, the *Ordo Templi Orientis* (O.T.O.), and gave him a charter† to found a camp‡ (local branch) of the O.T.O., which was at that time pretty much dead in England. Crowley, apparently taking into account Gardner's Masonic rank, granted him membership at that time (with or without initiations being performed or money changing hands) in the Fourth Degree of the O.T.O.'s eleven-degreed organization. By June, Gardner was a member of the Seventh Degree. Gardner became sick and went to America for a few months. While he was there, visiting with his younger brother in Memphis, Tennessee (and taking a look at Voodoo in New Orleans), Crowley died (on December 1, 1947). After Crowley's death, Gardner (promoting himself to the Tenth Degree, as befitted a national head of the order) apparently spent at least a year trying to revive the moribund British O.T.O., before giving it up to concentrate on his Witchcraft project instead.

---

*Founder of the religion of Thelema, scoundrel guru, and channeler of ancient Egyptian deities. See my discussion of him in *The Pagan Man* and *The Eye in the Triangle* by Israel Regardie.

†Which can be seen online at www.geraldgardner.com, which has a number of fascinating and scholarly essays on the history of the man and his religion.

‡Not, as Gardner claimed at one point later, to be the head of the O.T.O. in Europe, although if he had succeeded with his camp he might have become *de facto* head.

Crowley *may* also have given Gardner some after-the-fact permission to use bits of his poetry and ritual materials, which Gardner had been doing for years* and certainly continued doing in any event, leading to claims years later by critics that Gardner had paid Crowley to write the *Book of Shadows* for him. This last term, often abbreviated as *BOS*, was the name Gardner gave to his magical, initiatory, and pseudohistorical text. As some folks have said, this charge is ridiculous on the face of it, for if Crowley had written all the rituals in the *BOS* for Gardner, all the poetry would have been *much* better (Gerald wasn't much of a poet) and the structure of the ceremonies would have been much more complex and fancy.

Lance Sieveking (1897–1972), a British writer and journalist, in his autobiography *The Eye of the Beholder,* claims that in 1922 Montague Summers (1880–1948), author of several credulous books on werewolves, vampires, and the Inquisition, told him that Crowley and he were "both honorary members of several of the best covens" and had attended "many a sabbat" together. Oddly, there is no mention of this unusual membership or activity in Crowley's obsessively detailed and thoroughly shameless diaries, which are otherwise quite blasé about many ideas and activities that even today are shocking to some, such as his trisexuality (he'd "tri" anything sexual) and drug use.

There is an old rumor (still being told today) that Crowley had been "kicked out of" covens for refusing to obey their priestesses. This story was started by Gardner himself, and is mentioned by him in a letter to Cecil Williamson in 1950.* It was retold by Doreen

---

*Almost all of the Crowley material in *Ye Bok of Ye Art Magical* seems to have been taken from the "Blue Equinox" edition (Volume III, Number 1, 1919) of Crowley's magazine/book series *The Equinox* and his *Magick in Theory and Practice* (1929).

*Letter from Gardner to Williamson, dated February 8, 1950; footnoted in Morgan Davis's "From Man to Witch: Gerald Gardner 1946–1949," a brilliant essay that can be found at www.geraldgardner.com. I am indebted to Davis for some eye-opening details of these missing years of Gardner's life.

Valiente (1922–1999) to Gerald Yorke (another British occultist) in 1953, then by Gardner again in 1954, in his *Witchcraft Today*. This tale was also picked up by some of Gardner's less-scrupulous competitors, who were trying to assert the existence of pre-Gardner, priestess-led covens. When the Wiccan author Gavin Frost (founder, with his wife, Yvonne, of the Church and School of Wicca) asked Louisa Leek (mother of the famous astrologer and witch Sybil Leek), who was a friend of Crowley's, about these stories, he tells me, "She laughed her head off. [She said,] 'Crowley could never have stood the middle-aged housewife types that were in the later covens.' Apparently, he held out for the young, succulent, and intelligent."

Today, there remains *zero* evidence that Crowley had any conscious hand in the creation of Gardner's religion of Witchcraft, or its rituals, and even less that he had ever been initiated into or practiced *any* form of witchcraft. He would have cheerfully bragged about them if he had! The people who invented these tales were simply, to use the technical historical term again, *lying*.

Gardner's Crotona associates may have been, as he claimed, members of a surviving coven of Fam-Trad Witches. Or they may have been, as Fred Lamond, Gavin Frost, Ronald Hutton, and others believe, just a motley assortment of British occultists who had decided to create a new religion based on the books of Murray, Frazer, Leland, and other folklorists (to which Gardner would add the ideas of romantic poets, nudists, nature lovers, and believers in the myth of Merrie Olde England). Indeed, there apparently were several groups of British occultists, with overlapping memberships—England *is* a very small island—who were attempting to (re-)create Murray's theorized religion of Pagan Witchcraft at the same time. One of these, of which Louisa Leek was a member, was called the Pentagram Club and drew its membership from people in the Oxford and Cambridge academic communities. Another group, whose name I am not at liberty to reveal, seems to have been organized by some high-ranking members of the British nobility, who liked Murray's ideas of a royal connection to witchcraft.

One amusing tale, which might shed a bit of light on Gardner's sense of humor, has to do with the woman who supposedly was the "high priestess" of the New Forest Coven, Dorothy Clutterbuck (1880–1951), also known as "Old Dorothy." Much fuss has been made in recent years about the fact that she has been shown to have actually existed (Doreen Valiente, whom we'll meet later, tracked her life down).* While zero evidence has been discovered to indicate that she was a witch under any definition, Philip Heselton, in *Wiccan Roots,*† does argue that she was involved in Theosophy, Rosicrucianism, and Co-Masonry. Nonetheless, her existence has been used as "proof" that "Gardner *didn't* make it all up," and that therefore the coven must have existed as described by Gardner (and dualistically, that *everything* he said about it must therefore also be true). I have it on what I consider good authority (a British Wiccan who was around in the early days) that Gardner was having a bit of a joke by naming this very conservative, upper-middle-class woman as his high priestess. According to my source, "She would have been horrified at the thought that anyone could even conceive of her dancing naked in the woods with a bunch of witches!"

But whether or not he had any "authority" to do so, from an ancient coven that may or may not have existed (and may or may not have been ancient), Gerald Gardner founded his own coven during World War II (or shortly thereafter) and went merrily on his way. The war, unfortunately, had a devastating effect on occultism in Europe. The Nazis exterminated at least half the Romany people in Europe, along with many astrologers, psychics, Freemasons, Rosicrucians, Theosophists, Spiritualists, and other members of minority belief systems. By 1940, if any of the postulated Fam-Trad Witches had been left in Europe, few would have survived, precisely because they had been known as being those kinds of occultists.

*She published the results of her research as an appendix in Janet & Stewart Farrar's *The Witches' Way,* and in her *Witchcraft for Tomorrow* (1982).

†*Wiccan Roots: Gerald Gardner and the Modern Witchcraft Revival,* by Philip Heselton, 2000.

In 1948, Robert Graves (1895–1985) published *The White Goddess*. Up to this point, would-be witchcraft reconstructionists had mostly been following the works of Leland, Frazer, and Murray, all of whom were at least attempting to be scholarly and scientific, albeit heavily influenced by the academic fashions of their time (unlike modern scholars who are, naturally, immune to such subcultural biases). Now Graves, a writer of historical novels, a classicist, and a romantic poet, jumped into the act. The results were not pretty—or rather, that's all they were.

The purpose of *The White Goddess* was to prove that the Universal Goddess Worship theories the early anthropologists and archeologists had come up with were correct. To accomplish this took considerable acrobatics. He jumped back and forth from the Mediterranean to the British Isles and across great gaps of time. He constantly asked his readers to accept a "slight" bit of illogic and error, then built these up into gigantic megaliths of theory. While admitting he spoke no Celtic language, he appointed himself an authority on Welsh language and customs. He used obsolete and inaccurate translations of Celtic poetry, when there were good ones around in 1948, perhaps because the accurate translations wouldn't have supported his ideas as well.

In his defense, I should mention that Graves apparently wrote *The White Goddess* in a white-hot frenzy of inspiration in only a few weeks, while living at his summer home on the Isle of Malta, without his reference library.* He didn't claim that the book was a work of scholarship, but many people proceeded to treat it as if it were as reliable as his previous writings had been.

Graves's enthusiasm for the idea that all goddesses are either "Maidens," "Mothers," or "Crones" had a major effect on what would become the "duotheology" (see appendix 2) of the Mesopagan Witchcraft movement—and left a number of goddesses quite miffed, or so they have said during various "drawings down" (see chapter 15). Unfortunately, Graves, like Murray, is a good example of what I call

---

*As I have heard the story, there were some psychedelic substances involved too.

the "Retired Professor syndrome," in which a perfectly competent academic retires, gets bored, and decides to write a book on something he or she knows nothing about—with embarrassingly bad results, at least as far as the scholarship is concerned. Alas, they often sell far better than their previous academic works, thus encouraging further publications in the same line.

In 1949, Gardner published another bad novel, *High Magic's Aid,* under the pen name of Scire ("knower"), spelled incorrectly as Scrire. He apparently wanted to advertise that he was a member of a magical order, since the note "4°=7°" appears under his name, indicating to some that he had reached the level of "Philosophus" in the OTO. It appears, however, that "4°=7°" is a Golden Dawn or AA (Crowley's private magical order, rather than the 12 Step Program) degree, not an OTO one. Perhaps Gardner wanted people to assume that he had a solid background in the Golden Dawn and tantric-based OTO system of occult theory and practice, or perhaps he was sincerely studying them and intended to integrate them into his Witchcraft religion. Or it might have been a typesetter's error or a marketing ploy. No one at this point knows.

*High Magic's Aid* is the story of two young men who encounter a ceremonial magician and a witch and are initiated by the latter into a very Murrayite version of the Craft. In it we can see versions of what would become the standard Wiccan initiations, mixed with a great deal of ceremonial magic, most of it from the famous *Key of Solomon.*

In 1951, the British Witchcraft Act (intended for those who "pretended" to be witches) and the Vagrancy Act (aimed mostly at "Gypsies" and other traveling diviners who were assumed to be frauds) were both repealed (along with all the previous witchcraft laws in England) and a variety of "witches" surfaced. The most famous of these was the previously mentioned Sybil Leek, who claimed to be a Fam-Trad Witch (she may actually have been one—if only by one generation—if we consider her mother's supposed activities with the Pentagram Club's system of witchcraft).

In 1951, Gardner moved to the Isle of Man, settling into a building known as the Witches Mill, and running Cecil Williamson's Folklore Centre of Superstition and Witchcraft there as the "resident witch." Since Gardner had come to believe that a priestess must lead every coven, he began initiating likely candidates, and in 1953 he initiated Doreen Valiente. This turned out to be one of his best decisions, as she became more or less the Mother of Wicca.

Valiente rewrote most of Gardner's early ritual materials, dumping much of the early borrowings from Crowley, whom she personally loathed. Opinions among those who have read the earliest materials and her revisions are mixed as to whether her replacements for the Crowley material were actually better, but there is no doubt that she was a better poet than Gardner was. Later, she wrote her own excellent books, including *An ABC of Witchcraft Past and Present* (1973) and *Witchcraft for Tomorrow* (1988). After she left the coven, Gardner worked with several other women as priestesses, including Patricia Crowther (an author of several books, including *Lid off the Cauldron, Witches Were for Hanging,* and *High Priestess*), Monique Wilson, Eleanore ("Ray") Bone, and others.

From the mid-1950s on, new covens split off from Gerald's original one, both legitimately, through the process known as "hiving-off," wherein a Third-Degree woman with other members leave amicably with permission to begin a new coven, and illegitimately, through the process known as "stealing a copy of the *Book of Shadows.*"

Many versions of texts claiming to be from Gardner's original *Book of Shadows* have been published at one time or another, either by Gardner himself, by his followers and spiritual descendants, or by various plagiarists trying to cash in on his work. Gardner himself sent (badly) typewritten copies of his early drafts of rituals for the holidays, poems, and theological meditations to his initiates, asking for corrections and advice on whether the material "felt right."

It should be noted that there is no such thing as "the" Gardnerian *Book of Shadows!* This is true not only because Gardner was constantly changing his own copies but also because every Gardnerian initiate is supposed to be encouraged to add new materials and to pass these down to her or his own students in turn (with everything noted as to author and date of addition). So, no two copies of the *BOS* are identical and no one will ever be able to publish a "complete" edition.

Gardner's organizational vision of Witchcraft was of a structured system with elders knowing more than newcomers, but with the members considering each other as more or less equals, in keeping with Murray's idea that Witchcraft was a "peasant religion" (but contradicting Murray's other idea that it was connected to royalty). His earliest initiation scripts, as seen in his novel *High Magic's Aid*, had each member being labeled a "priest (or priestess) and witch" at his or her very first "degree." Gardner had borrowed the Masonic pattern—and much of the scripts—of three "degrees" of initiation. However, he soon discovered the "ninety-ten" rule common to most organizations, large or small: 90 percent of the work gets done by 10 percent of the members (while 90 percent of the complaining is done by a different 10 percent). So he soon had to invent the terms "High Priest" and "High Priestess" for the people actually fulfilling leadership roles.

The first splitting of Gardner's coven was when his priestess (Valiente) left with almost all the members and formed her own coven, with Gardner's acquiescence if not his approval. Soon, the term "hiving-off" was coined, on the metaphor of young female bees leaving a successful hive with a few males to start new hives. Eventually, the High Priestess of a coven that had experienced successful hivings-off was known as a "Witch Queen" (again, working with the bee metaphor). In a royalist nation, that was bound to cause problems, but not as many as it was to cause later in democratic countries.

The first hiving happened because Valiente and the others were opposed to the increasingly lurid interviews Gardner was giving to the British tabloid press (note to most Americans: these made—and make today—the *National Enquirer* look like the *New York Times*).

Ironically, just such a lurid interview had attracted Valiente's attention to Gardner in the first place! Doreen and company also disapproved of some of the women Gerald was initiating (he did have a sweet tooth for young, attractive women).

I can offer two arguments in Gardner's defense here. (1) A stronger than average libido is extremely common among both male and female founders of new religions throughout history,* and (2) I believe he was working on what we could today call a "Witches' Pyramid†Scheme." By initiating as many young people as possible, and encouraging all his initiates to do the same, he hoped that out of the large numbers who would eventually be initiated, enough of them would prove to have been good choices and would be able to keep his religion going.

This strategy worked surprisingly well. For example, one of Gardner's daughter covens initiated a couple named Rosemary and Raymond Buckland to all three degrees. The initiations happened in a relatively short time, but this was (and still is) common in Masonic and other fraternal lodges, so Gardner allowed and encouraged quick initiations. The Bucklands then went to the United States and founded a coven in Long Island, New York. This coven became the source of one of the most distinguished (and prolific) of all the Gardnerian "family lines" of initiates in the United States. Indeed, it's the line in which I eventually received my own Gardnerian Wiccan initiations.‡

When the Bucklands divorced sometime later, Rosemary got custody of the coven and quickly handed the High Priestess position down to another woman in the group. This left Raymond Buckland in a tight spot, for under the rules that had by then been created, a

---

*I won't list any of them here since some of their modern followers can get quite violent if you "insult" the founder by saying he / she had many lovers or spouses. For a Neopagan founder, however, it's practically a job requirement!

†"The Witches' Pyramid" is in reality a Wiccan meditation focused on the old occult phrase, "To know, to will, to dare, and to keep silent."

‡Not that I'm biased, of course.

High Priestess must preside at all initiations. Buckland also believed that Gardnerian covens had become "tyrannical" (I suspect that says something about his relationship with Rosemary). So he invented Seax (or "Saxon") Wica (he chose the alternate spelling that Gardner himself used) as an admittedly new denomination—or "Tradition" as all such new sects became known—into which anyone could initiate him- or herself.* That let the rabbit out of the hutch and apparently she was already pregnant! Buckland's stamp of approval on self-initiation set off a population explosion of Wiccan Witches. Meanwhile, other initiates of Gardner's various High Priestesses and daughter covens took his religion to Canada, Europe, Australia, South Africa, and elsewhere around the world.

The groups that were started by stealing copies of Gardner's *BOS* commonly claimed, as did members of other competing Witchcraft revivals/inventions in England, to belong to traditions of religious Witchcraft that predated Gardner's efforts. Yet somehow almost all of them wound up using rituals, customs, and vocabulary that were obviously derived from early drafts of Gardner's—I know, I've seen those drafts.

One of the early competitors, Robert Cochrane (1931–1966, also known as Roy Bowers),[†] was the former initiate who in 1964 started referring to Gardner's new religion as "the Gardnerian Tradition" or "Gardnerianism," in contrast to his own group, which he called "Traditional Witchcraft." Gardner himself called it by several different names over the years, including "the Art," "the Craft", "the Old Order," and "Wica" (with a single "c"). Eventually just about everyone settled on the last term, restoring the missing second "c" and making "Wicca" (pronounced with a "k" sound) the more or less of-

*He described this new Tradition in 1973 in a work called *The Tree,* recently released in an updated edition as *Buckland's Book of Saxon Witchcraft.*

[†]For more about him, see *Witchcraft: A Tradition Renewed,* by Evan John Jones (1999, with an Introduction by Doreen Valiente) and Jones's *The Roebuck in the Thicket: An Anthology of the Robert Cochrane Witchcraft Tradition* (2002) and *The Robert Cochrane Letters* (2003) by Cochrane, edited by Jones.

ficial generic term for what was to eventually become Neopagan Witchcraft (see below).

The first and most famous of those to schism from Gerald was Alex Sanders (1926–1988), who was later to make a career for himself as the purported "King of the Witches." Some have said that Alex's initiation was "not valid" since a First-Degree priestess rather than one who held the Second Degree gave it to him. Lamond says:

> As if that mattered! Alex was a natural medium and had been practicing ceremonial magic for a considerable time before his entry into Wicca, which is why he imported more kabbalistic practices into his tradition than there are in Gardnerian Wicca. Like many ceremonial magicians who practice too much . . . he had lost the ability to distinguish between planes of reality and really believed the whoppers he told people, like being initiated on the kitchen floor at the age of six by his grandmother.

Robert Cochrane claimed his coven pre-dated Gardner's and some of Cochrane's followers in the highly varied "1734 Tradition" still claim that today. Doreen Valiente was initiated into Cochrane's "Clan of Tubal Cain" in 1964, but did not stay. She did, however, contribute an introduction to Evans John Jones's book about the Cochrane tradition, *Witchcraft: A Tradition Renewed.*

At some point, Alex Sanders or someone from his coven initiated (probably to the Second Degree only, and probably by mail) an American woman named Jessie Wicker Bell (1920–2002). As "Lady Sheba" (calling oneself Lord or Lady when one became the High Priest or Priestess of a coven became a custom among Wiccans), she published *Lady Sheba's Book of Shadows* (1971) and the *Grimoire of Lady Sheba* (1972), through her friend and initiate, Carl Weschke, who happened to own the New Age publishing house Llewellyn Publications. Her books launched the Pagan publishing boom of the 1970s, leading to Llewellyn becoming an 800-pound gorilla and placing books about Wicca and other Neopagan paths into thousands of bookstores throughout the English- and Spanish-speaking world. Unfortunately, Bell's books simply plagiarized (and garbled) parts of Gardner's *BOS* (a popular sport for a few decades) along with material from Gavin Frost and Yvonne Frost's Church and School of Wicca correspondence course (as have a surprising number of other supposedly authentic holders of Ancient Wiccan Traditions). Her attempts in the early 1970s to get herself declared "Queen of the Witches" in America met with little success, however (see the next chapter).

I cannot in this short study give an adequate history of how Gardner's followers and competitors carried the faith(s) to America and elsewhere. Suffice it to say that by the mid-1960s there were a handful of Gardnerian (and other "British Traditional") covens operating in the United States and Canada and other parts of the English-speaking world. By the 1970s, there were dozens more independent Traditions/denominations of Wicca flourishing throughout the English-speaking world. Both Aidan Kelly's *Crafting the Art of Magic*, though severely flawed, and Margot Adler's classic *Drawing Down the Moon* cover this material well (at least for the United States and Canada). The growth in numbers of Traditions and their members since has been astronomical.

The many current varieties of Wicca can be ranged on a spectrum of orthodoxy to heterodoxy thusly: on the conservative or orthodox side we will find:

- Gardnerians
- Alexandrians
- Other groups that call themselves "British Traditionalists"

Groups that would be on the liberal or heterodox end of the spectrum would include:

- The New Reformed Orthodox Order of the Golden Dawn (NROOGD; a Wiccan tradition proudly self-invented in Berkeley, California, in the 1960s, which chose a silly sounding name to keep out people with no sense of humor)

- The gay and/or bisexual and/or straight groups who call themselves "Elvish" or "Fairy/Faery" Traditions (see appendix 3)
- Various Feminist Witchcraft groups discussed in chapter 10

Most Wiccan groups, of course, fall somewhere in between the
two ends of this spectrum. Many on both ends like to create a di-
chotomy (often a dualism) between the so-called "Traditionalists,"
who are the members of conservative groups with a legitimate (or
purported) lineage back to Gardner or other supposed pre-Gardner
British covens, and the "Eclectics," who are liberal in their practices,
following the technique of using anything that works no matter where
it comes from.

Some Wiccan groups cheerfully call themselves Eclectic, but the
word is often used by the conservatives to imply that the liberals don't
have the Real Truth and have to make things up as they go along (as
if that were a crime). Similarly, the liberals often use the word
"Traditionalist" to mean "stuffy and rigid." The vast majority of Wiccans are neither religiously conservative nor liberal (on this particular
spectrum), but somewhere in the middle, so in keeping with the
principles of Western dualism, they are usually accused by Wiccans at
each extreme of belonging to the "enemy's" camp.

Beyond all the arrogance and egotism of these arguments, the primary difference between the eclecticism practiced by both the orthodox and the heterodox Wiccans, going all the way back to Gardner
himself, is not the *amount* of material borrowed from other sources,
but the *speed* at which new material is accepted as a permanent part of
each Tradition/denomination. Eclectic groups may invent a new custom or borrow it from another group and immediately incorporate it
as part of its system. Traditionalists may do something quite similar,
but try it out for a few years before considering it to be "traditional"
and inscribing it into their *BOS*.

I should point out that this chapter—indeed all of this book—is
greatly indebted for the clarification of the Gardner-Crowley relationship, as well as much else in the complex background of Wicca's

creation, to Ronald Hutton's magnificent work *The Triumph of the Moon: A History of Modern Pagan Witchcraft*. This meticulously documented book by a sympathetic historian pounds the final nails into the coffin of the claims Gardner made (and others inflated) that Wica/Wicca was an ancient British Pagan religion of Witchcraft, surviving from the Middle Ages if not the Stone Age.

Of course, his work has been dismissed by those who loathe scholarship, at least when it treads on their preferences, and some have been quick to say that academic fashions change, so that it might be possible for later historians to completely overthrow Hutton's work. Well, yes, but historians have agreed for quite some time that the Roman Empire came before the British one and that Benjamin Franklin invented the lightning rod. Some historical ideas are unlikely to change without dramatic new evidence being presented, which the supporters of an ancient origin for Wicca refuse to provide. Those scholars who have looked at the history of Wicca have examined hundreds of pieces of evidence that fit together like a jigsaw to present a clear, if incomplete, picture of how Gardner, Valiente, and others synthesized the Craft out of dozens of known sources.

None but the most stubbornly orthodox Wiccans can deny Wicca's true history any longer, though I'm sure that some of them will continue to try. Valiant efforts have been made, by Valiente in *Witchcraft for Tomorrow* and others such as Phillip Heselton, the author of *Wiccan Roots*, to prove that some of the people Gardner referred to as members of his source coven really lived. Unfortunately, as Gardner's joke about Clutterbuck shows, knowing that these people may have lived tells us nothing about whether or not they considered themselves witches and whether the New Forest Coven was 6, 60, or 600 years old when Gardner supposedly encountered it in 1939.

By the way, Hutton and Heselton do not disagree quite as much as many seem to think. While I was writing this update, Hutton told me in an e-mail that

I fear that most people—or at least most people in North America—seem to get their impressions of Philip Heselton's books at second- or third-hand. From the comments that I receive across the Atlantic, these impressions never seem to include the information that I contributed supportive prefaces to both books, and that both include a tribute to me for the help that I gave to Philip in the research. The concept does not seem to exist among a lot of Canadian and American Pagans that authors with different views of a subject can actually co-operate in the study of it.

See Ashleen O'Gaea's comments in appendix 7 for a detailed review of Hutton's work and some conclusions similar to those I've expressed here.

# PART THREE

# NEOPAGAN WITCHCRAFT

# CHAPTER 9

# The First Neopagan Witches—and the First Neopagan Heretics

henever mind-altering drugs become common in a culture or subculture, one of the common social repercussions is a renewed interest in matters magical and mystical. I'm speaking mostly of opiates and hallucinogens here, not alcohol, tobacco, caffeine, or refined sugar (which most Americans pretend are not "really" drugs) or legal pharmaceuticals such as tranquilizers, antidepressants, or stimulants (which we pretend aren't mind-altering). Natural drugs of many varieties are used in many tribal cultures to help train young magicians/clergy, because they give the trainee a direct appreciation of the magical Law of Infinite Universes (the idea that sensory experiences can be organized into an infinite number of possible "universes") and the related concept of "multiple levels of reality." Drugs are used as sacraments in many magical and religious systems around the world and an interest in either topic (drugs or magic) can lead to an interest in the other.

So it should have surprised no one that many of the "hippies" of the 1970s, who experimented with marijuana, LSD, mescaline, and other drugs, became interested in magic, mysticism, psychic phenomena, and new religious experiences. For that matter, it should have surprised no one familiar with the history of monotheism that early psychedelic researchers such as Timothy Leary (1920–1996)

would be treated as horrifically threatening "heretics" and demonized in the mass media.

Although Leary was often referred to as a "drug guru" by the tabloid press, he really had little interest in starting a religion. Others, however, were more enthusiastic (in the original sense of "breathed through by deities"). During the 1960s and '70s, several new religious groups (such as the Church of the Eternal Source, Feraferia, and the Church of All Worlds*) were started that collectively become known by their members as "Neopagan." Each attempted to re-create or invent new religions using the Paleopagan polytheistic faiths as guides, but with an Aquarian Age disregard for monotheistic and dualistic assumptions. Gerald Gardner's religion of Pagan Witchcraft, with its Goddess, Horned God, and other spirits, fit very nicely into this mold. As a result, the followers of Gardner experienced an unexpected and not altogether welcome population explosion as the handful of Gardnerian covens (real and imitation) became a dozen, then a score, then a hundredscore.

During the 1960s and '70s, members of a variety of Neopagan groups were communicating via the pages of amateur periodicals such as *Green Egg, Waxing Moon, Crystal Well*, and others (see Margot Adler). Soon it became clear to the members of these groups that the Wiccans were Neopagans—or "could be with a little work"—and they and their offshoots were called "Neopagan Witches" by the rest of the Neopagan movement. This really annoyed those Wiccans (most of them at the time) who believed that there was nothing "neo-" about them—how could you be new if you belonged to the "Old Religion"?—and weren't even sure they wanted to be called "Pagans" of any sort (the terms "Paleo-" and "Mesopagan" hadn't been invented yet).

By this time the "Myth of Wicca" had jelled and these newly dubbed "Neopagan Witches" began to hold conventions and other

---

*See my book *The Pagan Man* and Margot Adler's *Drawing Down the Moon* for details.

meetings. At one of the earliest of these, a "Witchmeet" held in Minneapolis, Minnesota, on September 20–23, 1973, hosted by Llewellyn Publications (later to become the largest publisher of Wiccan and other Neopagan books), three important events for the history of American Wicca took place.

First, Lady Sheba, claiming an ancient Family Tradition of Witchcraft going back to the mythical Isle of Avalon, attempted to be recognized as the true hereditary Queen of all American Witches (because her family had supposedly been the hereditary Queens of all British Witches). Not incidentally, she wanted everyone present to turn over copies of their *Books of Shadows* to her. As I recall, her intention was to combine them into a single "approved" *BOS* for all American Witches; much like the event in early Christian history when "authorized" scriptures were approved by a group of bishops based in Rome and "unauthorized" copies (with inconvenient stories and doctrines) were carefully destroyed. To her chagrin, Lady Sheba was firmly told by the assembled Wiccans that, "We're a democracy in this country—we don't need a Queen!"*

Second, the Council of American Witches was created. This short-lived group was to meet the following spring and adopt its "Principles of Wiccan Belief," the first consensus document describing the Wiccan religion (see appendix 4).

Third, I gave a speech titled "The Witch Cult—Fact or Fancy?" based on an earlier article by myself in *Tournaments Illuminated*,† under the title "Where Hast Thou Been Sister?" It came to conclusions, similar to those we have been discussing, about what I much-too-rudely referred to as Margaret Murray's "Unitarian Universalist White Witch-Cult of Western Theosophical Brittany," as mostly being illogical nonsense, and Gardner's supposed revival of it as having been mostly his own creation.

Stunned silence, then angry shouting greeted my speech. I was

---

*I must confess, I believe I was the first person to actually be rude enough to say that out loud.

†The journal of the medievalist Society for Creative Anachronism.

seriously snubbed by many of the attending Wiccans and witches-
with-a-small-w for the rest of the event. This major miffedness turned
into a roar of anger and hostility after the speech was published (sans
the bibliography, alas!) in *Gnostica News,* Llewellyn's in-house magazine, which I was later to edit. Thus, as a reward for my attempted
scholarship, I became the first recognized heretic in the Neopagan
movement—or at least among the Wiccans and the witches.

Rebuttals to my arguments were written and published in
*Gnostica News,* and angry letters poured in to the Neopagan media
from all over the country, until slowly, one by one, various Wiccans
began to publish letters and articles saying, in essence, "that so-and-so
Bonewits is right about Wicca not being ancient," though hardly any
of them mentioned my name. Instead, they talked about the need for
honesty in relating the past of Wicca, about the joys of creating new
religions, about how their movement could be redefined as a "recon-
struction"* from scattered fragments of how the Old Religions (plural
now) might have been, and so on.

However, yet another significant event in the history of Wicca occurred at about the same time. This was in 1974 or 1975, early into
my career as editor of *Gnostica News.* I was supervising the publica-
tion of an article by Aidan Kelly (a founder of the NROOGD
Wiccan Tradition in California) called "Textual Criticism and the
Craft Laws," in which he had applied the techniques of biblical textual analysis to compare previously published versions of what
Gardner had called the "Ancient Laws of the Craft." This document
purported to be a set of rules that the supposed medieval Pagan
witches had used to guide their religion and protect themselves from
the unholy Inquisition.

Carl Weschke, the owner of Llewellyn Publications, while discussing this article with me in his office, suddenly remembered some
documents that had been sent to him by a person claiming to be one

---

*Of course, you can't reconstruct something that never existed in the first place,
but nevermind.

of Gardner's early initiates. With the offhand comment, "Perhaps these might be interesting to you," he handed me a set of papers, which his correspondent had said Gardner himself had mailed to him for comments many years before.

My jaw slowly dropped as I realized that I was holding carbon (and "NCR paper"*) copies of documents that had been typed by Gardner himself (I could tell by the characteristic use of the lower case "l" to substitute for his typewriter's broken capital "I"—years earlier I had received a letter from him typed that way). Furthermore, the documents appeared to be early drafts of some of the materials that Gardner had always claimed in public were old—including the Craft Laws! Quickly, I made duplicates of the documents and, with Weschke's permission, mailed a set to Kelly, so he could compare them to his previous research.

Those papers set Kelly on a path that ended in a complete revision of his theories. He had previously argued that the Craft Laws went back to at least the seventeenth century, based on comparing the published versions of them and working backward toward a hypothetical document that might have preceded all of them. He had been fooled, in large part, by Gardner's habit of plucking bits of Old and Middle English vocabulary from the *Oxford English Dictionary* and dropping them into his rituals and notes. Soon, Kelly was writing a book that would circulate in photocopies for nearly twenty years among American Wiccans, arguing that those same methods of textual criticism proved that Gardner had synthesized nearly all of his supposedly ancient writings from previously published materials by other authors and his own creativity.

In later years, Kelly discovered the document known as *Ye Bok*[†] *of Ye Art Magical,* forgotten at the back of a file cabinet full of Gardner's papers, then owned by the Ripley Museum in Toronto. *Ye Bok* was a

---

*That's the stuff that makes yellow and pink paper copies of surface originals that have been typed on.

[†]Yes, Gardner spelled it that way. I have been lucky enough to be able to examine *Ye Bok* myself, and it is exactly as Kelly described it.

hand-bound book in which Gardner had written, scratched out, and amended the very first drafts of what would eventually become the rituals for his new religion, surrounded by a lot of earlier material copied from various ceremonial magical books. This discovery provided even more evidence to support the conclusions Kelly had come to.

Kelly became the second Neopagan heretic, even more widely reviled than myself for casting doubts on the antiquity of Wicca, and his manuscript became the next-to-most famous and influential unpublished book about Wicca—second only to the theoretical "complete" Gardnerian *BOS* itself. Thus, it was all the more tragic that, when the manuscript was finally published as *Crafting the Art of Magic* in 1991, it was so drastically shortened, filled with internal Gardnerian political arguments (Kelly had become a Gardnerian initiate by then), and marred by repeated cheap shots at Gardner's (assumed) sexuality. I felt as if I had watched a friend paint a beautiful mural for twenty years, then throw mud all over it the night before it was revealed to the public.

But even before Kelly published his work, between the two of us and those Pagan scholars who followed, the Wiccan myth of antiquity had been thoroughly discredited. This was due in large part to Margot Adler's long interviews with the two of us and her discussion of our ideas in her amazing book *Drawing Down the Moon: Witches, Druids, Goddess-Worshippers, and Other Pagans in America Today.* Her work made it clear, even to those of us who had been Pagans for years, just how vibrant, creative, varied, and evolutionary our religious creations were and could be.

*Drawing Down the Moon** became a self-reflective handbook showing us options and resources that many of us had never previously known, combined with gentle warnings of how we could go wrong (such as by slipping into the psychological habits of the mainstream religions) if we weren't careful. Every Neopagan should own a copy!

The major religious issues fought over by the Wiccan and other

---

*A newly updated edition is in preparation.

Neopagan movements during the latter third of the twentieth century included those of hierarchy versus autonomy, the related issue of lineage (or "apostolic succession") versus self-initiation, and the question of sexism and heterosexism (or homophobia) in the Craft. Arguments raged over whether "Witch Queens" had any real or even appropriate authority over anyone other than members of covens descended from them (if then). People fought over whether "only a Witch can make another Witch" or if people could "legitimately" initiate themselves. Wiccans debated whether the heterosexual erotic imagery of the Goddess's and God's sacramental wedding (see chapter 15) constituted discrimination against homosexuals—for that matter, if homosexuals were even "allowed" to be Witches. Then they argued whether erotic activity performed in *some* orthodox Wiccan initiations should be seen as "sexual abuse" of the initiates by the initiators, even if the initiates were warned about it ahead of time, or if such warnings would, for the sake of being "politically correct," destroy the intended effect of the activity and thus invalidate the initiation!

Over the years, disputes over "allowable" or "forbidden" practices that were rooted in the alleged antiquity of the traditions (and Traditions) involved became of interest only to those decreasing numbers of Wiccans who still believed their founders' tales of unbroken connections going back to the Stone Age (or at least the Middle Ages). Everyone else made their religious decisions about these issues based on their other social, political, and sexual beliefs and practices, which were evolving along with the rest of postmodern culture.

CHAPTER 10

# Sisters Doing It for Themselves

To plagiarize poor Gerald can bring you much renown,
And it's easy when you merely take out every male noun.
If people did it to them, they would vilify the crooks,
But some think it fine and dandy for their feminist books!

ne of the most important influences on the evolution of religious Witchcraft was the rise of the feminist movement in the 1970s. Many feminists were looking for new sources of spiritual growth, away from the male-dominated "Great Religions of the World." This women's spirituality movement became an integral part of feminist consciousness for many women, some of whom, inevitably, ran into Neopagan Witches.

Morning Glory Zell-Ravenheart seems to have been the first Neopagan priestess to attend a major feminist event in the 1970s and to attempt to speak about "the Goddess" to the participants. Oddly enough, only one person—a man—showed up to listen to her, though her listing in the program booklet apparently affected many women who had never heard about Wicca previously.

Evidently, the discovery of a Goddess-worshiping religion in the late twentieth century was a delightful shock. Many women felt an immediate resonance and in ever-increasing numbers had spiritual experiences with this Goddess. Since there were already many Neopagan

Witches (of both genders) who considered themselves feminists—it's hard (though possible) to be a Goddess worshiper without being one—an alliance or overlap of the two movements was a natural outgrowth of their meeting.

A few Wiccan denominations had already downplayed the Horned God part of their duotheology almost to the point of removing Him from their religions entirely; perhaps these traditions had started with a high population of assertive women and passive men. When politically active feminists (especially lesbians and separatists) entered the Craft and started their own all-women covens, they decided that they could do perfectly well without any male deity at all and began developing "thealogies" (Goddess-centered theologies) focused exclusively on female deities.

Feminist Witchcraft was the result—systems of Wicca that became increasingly different from the Neopagan models, as various women (often with no real knowledge of or contact with the Neopagan movement) formed new sects, in which a great deal of experimentation and creativity took place.

Most Feminist Witches soon accepted several dogmas, the majority of which matched those of Neopagan Witchcraft before my speech of 1973, although even more extreme: the Universal Goddess Cult had supposedly covered the entire world, not just Europe; it went back 100,000 years (not just 10,000), and so forth. These dogmas were backed by research that was even sloppier than that done a hundred years earlier. Historical, semihistorical, or pseudohistorical statements or theories by any writer (male or female, qualified or not) that bolstered their dogmas were seized on and inflated. Statements or theories that did not support those dogmas were ignored, minimized as being the products of male (or worse, "male-dominated" female) minds, and/or were denounced as part of a millennia-old sexist conspiracy to suppress the Truth.

As more books were published in mainstream academia regarding the historical nonexistence of matriarchies, for example, the definition of "matriarchy" was simply changed to match whatever a speaker or writer wished it to mean. Often, the word was replaced by "matri-focal" (focused on mothers) or "woman-centered" or by various phrases indicating cultures in which the genders were more or less politically equal (for which there actually *are* a few historical examples).

The Feminist Craft grew (and may still be growing) at a rapid rate, and at this writing members of these groups might outnumber those of the Neopagan sects from which they diverged. The number of groups of women who have formed covens completely independently is impossible to surmise and their thealogies are no doubt quite mixed, but feminist revisionist "her-story" (a reaction to male-focused "his-story") is probably common to most.*

While the Neopagan Witches were slowly ceasing to claim literal truth for their mythic history, the Feminist Witches continued those same myths, and in fact made them more spectacular and rich—i.e., the patriarchal Christians overthrew the matriarchy 10,000 years ago. . . . It is only in the last decade or so that some Feminist Witches, such as Starhawk and Z Budapest, have begun to doubt these dog-mas, while continuing to look for better research to support less ex-treme claims. Perhaps it is finally becoming known that dozens of committed feminist historians, anthropologists, and archeologists of both genders have been unable to find a shred of evidence to sup-port the idea that matriarchies ever existed, that there was ever a Universal Goddess Cult, or that there ever was an organized religion of Witchcraft in Europe, and that the intact transmission of a com-plex pre-Christian tradition is not at all likely.

I suspect that the feminist movement ("It's not dead yet!") will continue to produce, as has every other political movement in his-tory, sloppily researched tomes in support of its ideals. There is, after all, no such thing as completely unbiased scholarship (no matter what some professors may claim) and feminists should be allowed to exer-cise their historical creativity as much as any other political group does.

*For example, see Merlin Stone's classic *When God Was a Woman*.

Within a decade or two, however, Feminist Witchcraft groups may well admit that their various sects are not ancient relics but the brilliant and beautiful creations of modern religious visionaries. Perhaps at that point they will be willing to consider themselves part of the larger Neopagan movement and its hundreds of thousands of Goddess-worshiping men and God-worshiping women.

# CHAPTER 11

# Witchcraft in the Postmodern World

o, what do we have in the way of modern witches at the dawn of the twenty-first century? There are those I've called Neoclassic Witches, who are herbalists, tarot card readers, and sometimes midwives, patterning themselves, consciously or unconsciously, after the Classic Witches I now prefer to call the Cunning Folk.

Even today, however, there are people we could call Neodiabolic Witches: modern Satanists who are trying their very best to be everything the Roman Catholic and Protestant churches said (and say) they should be. Fortunately, only a few crazies go so far as to perform human sacrifice like they are "supposed" to. Though they represent only a tiny percentage of the people now calling themselves witches, neodiabolics grab all the publicity they can get to present themselves as more important than they really are. Most modern Satanists, however, are far too arrogant to call themselves witches of any sort, preferring to describe themselves as "Satanic magicians" and such. More important, even though the infamous Church of Satan used the term "witch" to describe its first level of initiation back in the 1960s, most Satanists today don't consider what they do to be a religion at all, but rather a "philosophy."

Naturally, there are conservative Christian groups who are delighted to have the Neodiabolic Witches around to support their doctrine that "all witches worship the Devil." Some supposed ex-

Neodiabolic Witches are now making lucrative livings as traveling evangelists, denouncing their former (imaginary) ways. If you meet any of them, you might want to ask them and their audiences why they are not in prison, if they really committed all the awful crimes they claim. After all, secular law does not recognize a supposed "born again" experience as absolving criminals from paying for their crimes. And yet it always turns out that "the witch who switched" has never done a day of prison time for his or her imaginary atrocities.

We now even have some folks attempting to create forms of Neoshamanic Witchcraft, whether inspired by Morning Glory Zell-Ravenheart's theory (mentioned in chapter 3) or else just using the currently vague New Age concepts of shamanism combined with Wicca. It's ironic that, while authentic shamanism is about as nitty-gritty and practical as a magical system can get (shamans who don't produce reliable thaumaturgic results tend to get "fired," at the least) the modern (Neo-)Shamanic Witches tend to be the "fluffiest" of "fluffy bunny Pagans" (those delicate souls who believe in "Nature pink in gum and paw").

But the largest numbers by far, dwarfing those of all the other categories put together, are the overlapping communities of Neopagan and Feminist Witches, of whom there may well be over a million by now.

Defining who is or isn't a "real" member of these communities for statistical purposes is a complex task that changes the final tallies dramatically depending on the assumptions with which one starts. Nonetheless, our numbers will only grow in the coming decades, as our population seems (to us long-time observers) to have doubled in size every four or five years. Considering the many popular books about Wicca and Goddess Worship still filling the bookstore shelves long after the "fad" was supposed to be "over," I see no sign of this growth slowing down. The recent arrival of books about us in Spanish, French, Russian, and other languages indicates that this family of religions is just getting started!

For that matter, the increasing desperation of Catholic and fundamentalist Christian leaders to attack us as a demonic threat would seem to show that the dinosaurs have finally figured out who the mammals that are going to replace them are!

Let me stress that the relative youth of the Neopagan and Feminist Witchcraft movements, the deliberately vague and unorganized nature of our beliefs and institutions, and the personal moral failings of some of our founders are all utterly irrelevant to any judgment of spiritual power and worth for the religions as a whole. Can you imagine what scholars would have said about Judaism, Christianity, or Islam if they had been able to do this sort of historical analysis within each of those faiths' first century? Unlike the authorities of other major religions, Wiccans have neither the power nor the inclination to kill people for digging into our dirty laundry and have made no major efforts to destroy inconvenient bits of historical evidence, such as *Ye Bok*.

The deities we worship *are* ancient, no matter how new our religions or our insights about Them might be. A large part of the maturing of the Neopagan community over the past thirty years has been due to the realization that we don't have to tell fibs about an unbroken line of succession going back to the Stone Age to have worthwhile faiths.

As for how "unspiritual" our founders may seem, Fred Lamond told me:

> The reason Idries Shah took such interest in Gerald, to the extent of writing his biography, was [he said], "I have it on good authority (I assume he meant the inner planes [mystical levels of consciousness]) that this group is going to be the cornerstone of the religion of the coming age. But rationally (and he looked despairingly at us sincere but woefully ignorant young people), I can't see it!"

Ah, but we still younger folks have lived long enough to see it! Uncle Gerald, Aunt Doreen, and all the other dreamers, scholars, poets, and rakes working with them (and even sometimes against them) created a beautiful synthesis of ancient and modern religious, artistic, and magical archetypes, one that has grown and evolved into a huge family of emotionally satisfying and spiritually powerful belief systems.

During its first half-century, Wicca has been a beautiful dreamship riding the crest of the third wave of postmodern civilization. The past, whether seen as "his-story" or "her-story," is only the beginning.

# PART FOUR

# WICCAN BELIEFS
# AND
# RITUALS

# CHAPTER 12

# What Wiccans Believe

"It's true, it's true
We made it all up and it's true!" *

hile this is not the place for a full-scale discussion of Wiccan duotheology (the study of the Wiccan God and Goddess), this chapter will give you the highlights and make the subsequent chapters more meaningful. Because Wiccans *are* Neopagans, whether all of them are willing to admit it or not, much of this is taken from my essay "What Neopagans Believe," which I have rewritten many times over the years.[†]

Clarifying our doctrines (the things we do and don't believe) without descending into dogma (the things we are ordered to believe or disbelieve by someone in a position of power over us) is a vital step in the growth of any new religious movement. . . . Not everyone in the Neopagan movement will use the term "belief" in reference to these concepts and many of these concepts have a wide variety of accepted interpretation. Even so, it's reasonably easy to list those ideas with which a majority of us usually agree or disagree, and thus sketch the outlines of our doctrines.

---

*Unofficial motto of the New Reformed Orthodox Order of the Golden Dawn.
[†]Beginning in 1974 in *The Druid Chronicles (Evolved)*, which can be found at www.carleton.edu/mikerdna. The current version can be found on my website at www.neopagan.net/NeopagansBelieve.html.

Wiccans represent the vast majority of the Neopagan movement, and as such have affected the majority of the beliefs and practices of that movement. In the following, I list the beliefs as they are held by *most* Neopagans and add comments that are specific to Wiccan beliefs and practices. Be warned, however, that these are spiritual movements still very much in their early growth stages and that not all members of these movements may agree completely with any particular one of the beliefs I list.

Neopagans believe that *divinity is both immanent (internal) and transcendent (external)*. Deities can manifest at any point in space or time that They might choose, whether externally through apparent "visitations," or internally through the processes known as "inspiration," "conversation," "channeling," and "possession."

Neopagans believe that *children are born holy*, since they have no barriers of consciousness between their selves and their indwelling deities. So we believe in "original blessing" rather than "original sin" and we thus see no need for "salvation" from the latter. Because of this reverence for children, Wiccans and other Neopagans do *not* approve of any form of child abuse.

Neopagans believe that *divinity is as likely to manifest in a female form as it is in a male form* and that the word "Goddess" makes just as much sense as the word "God." Wiccans in particular believe that feminine energies and values are needed to balance the masculine excesses of current cultures. Women and men are spiritually equal, and "masculine" and "feminine" attitudes, values, and roles are of equal importance, regardless of the physical gender of those exercising them. However, some Wiccan traditions reserve certain ritual roles to one physical gender or the other.

Neopagans believe in a *multiplicity of gods and goddesses*, as well as "lesser" beings, many of Whom are worthy of respect, love, and worship. Neopagans have a wide variety of nonexclusive concepts as to the nature of these entities. Among Wiccans, female deities are usually seen as aspects or faces of a single "Triune" Goddess, most often described as a Maiden, a Mother, and a Crone. Male deities are likewise usually seen as aspects or faces of a single "Biune" God, most often described as a vegetation/hunting and solar deity but sometimes as an Oak King and Holly King as representatives of the summer and winter halves of the year. Thus, Wicca is predominantly "duotheistic." A significant minority worships only female deities, however.

Multiplicity of deities implies a multiplicity of truths, and vice versa, which leads most Neopagans to believe that *no one religion, philosophy, scripture, or other approach to understanding can explain the infinite complexities of the multiverse.* No one has a real monopoly on truth, only highly developed guesses and/or large armies.

Christian theologians call this concept of multiplicity of deities and truths an "open metaphysic" and find it terrifying. Because of the importance of divine immanence, personal experience can be just as important a source of truth as logic or reason—or someone's sacred scriptures—might be, each on different levels of reality.

Neopagans *do not believe in, respect, or worship any divine or semi-divine figure of ultimate Evil,* leaving such concepts to the dualistic monotheists. They invented Satan; they can keep him. As a demigod who was created by Christian and Islamic fear, Satan/Shaitan plays no part in Wiccan or other Neopagan beliefs and practices. As for all those "demons" that some Christians are so obsessed by, those few Wiccans who believe in them at all tend to see them as merely predatory species of spirits in the astral bioregions, who are no more innately hostile to (or even interested in) humans than rattlesnakes or scorpions are.

Most Neopagans believe *it is necessary to respect and love Nature as divine in Her own right* and *to accept ourselves as part of Nature and not Her "rulers."* Many accept the "Gaia thesis," that the Earth's biosphere is a living being. Gaia can be seen as the ultimate Earthly face of the Goddess as the Divine Mother. In some senses, this can be seen as a kind of animism ("everything has a spirit"), pantheism ("the divine is everywhere"), or panentheism ("the divine is in everything").

Neopagans believe that *ethics and morality should be based on joy, love, self-esteem, mutual respect, and the avoidance of actual harm to others and ourselves.* Most Neopagans believe in some variant of the principle of "karma" and affirm that the results of their actions will always return to them, sooner or later. Many Wiccans go so far as to believe that their karmic return will be three times as strong, for good or ill, as what their actions unleashed.

Neopagans believe that *human beings were meant to lead lives filled with joy, love, pleasure, beauty, and humor.* Neopagans may be carnivores, vegetarians, or omnivores, depending on their individual religious beliefs. Some Neopagans abstain from alcoholic beverages, but most neither abstain nor disapprove of others drinking

Most Neopagans believe that *sexual ecstasy is a divine blessing* and that *it can be a major source of spiritual growth and enlightenment,* though we vary widely in how, with whom, and under what circumstances we seek such ecstasy. Indeed, Gerald Gardner's original vision of Wicca was that it was to be a sex magic movement rooted in a westernization of Hindu and Buddhist Tantric practices. Because Neopagans are sympathetic toward many sexual minorities and alternative relationship styles that have been persecuted by monotheistic religions, we attract many of them.

Neopagans believe that *with proper training, art, discipline, and intent, human minds and hearts are fully capable of performing most of the magic and miracles they are ever likely to need.* The performance of magic is a central practice in Wicca, as is divination. This belief clashes directly with monotheistic claims to exclusive miraculous abilities for their founders and saints, as well as their clergy's demands for exclusive "rights" to perform paranormal acts.

Neopagans believe in *the importance of celebrating the solar, lunar, and other cycles of our lives.* We consciously observe the solstices, equinoxes, and the points in between, as well as the phases of the moon and the passages of our lives.

Most Neopagans believe in *some sort of afterlife as well as reincarnation,* usually involving rest and recovery in the "Summerland" (a term taken from Spiritualism) before reincarnating. There is a common belief that we grow spiritually through each lifetime and will continue reincarnating until we have learned all we need to.

There isn't much of a developed duotheology of the afterlife in most Wiccan denominations, so questions about who goes to the Summerland, vs. who reincarnates (immediately or after some metaphysical R&R), vs. what happens to really evil people, etc., just aren't talked about much. Wiccans, like many other Neopagans, pay more attention to this life than to any hypothesized afterlife and tend to consider the concept of eternal torture or reward a key sign of dysfunctional religions.

Neopagans believe that if we are to achieve any of our goals, *we must practice what we preach.* Neopaganism, like any other religion, should be a way of life. Hence the popular Wiccan saying: "The Craft is not a Hobby."

Most Neopagans believe that *healthy religions should have a minimum amount of rigidity and a maximum amount of flexibility.* Wicca, like the rest of Neopaganism, is an assortment of organic religions, which are growing, changing, merging, splitting, and producing offshoots.

Neopagans believe in *freedom of worship and belief* for all religious groups and individuals who are willing to grant us our freedoms in return—not always an easy agreement to get from other faiths—and in withholding social support for those who are bigots. We see religious tolerance as a sign of spiritual strength and confidence.

With all this as background, and remembering that for many Wiccans and other Neopagans these beliefs are thought of more as metaphors and artistic designs than as "doctrines," let's take a brief look at the different kinds of rituals that Wiccans practice.

# CHAPTER 13

# Varieties of Wiccan Ritual

cholars in the field of religious studies often call Wicca and other varieties of Neopaganism "magical religions." By this they mean to indicate faiths in which the participants are encouraged and expected to actively perform their own magical or "miraculous" deeds, rather than passively waiting for some spiritual force to do it for them. Down through the ages the core meaning of "witch" has been someone who could do "magic." Yet what exactly do we mean by that?

Defining magic (or "magick" as those who want to disassociate themselves from the way stage magic is spelled) is a long and complex task. I'll refrain from repeating my long discussion of this in *Real Magic* (1971/1989) and *Authentic Thaumaturgy*. (1979/1999). Here are the three definitions I normally use for "magic":

1. A general term for arts, sciences, philosophies, and technologies concerned with (a) understanding and using various altered states of consciousness within which it is possible to have access to and control over one's psychic talents, and (b) the uses and abuses of those psychic talents to change interior and/or exterior realities.

2. A science and art comprising a system of concepts and methods for the buildup of human emotions, altering the electrochemical balance of the metabolism, and using associational techniques and devices to concentrate and focus this emo-

tional energy, thus modulating the energies broadcast by the human body, usually to affect other energy patterns whether animate or inanimate, but occasionally to affect the personal energy pattern.

3. A collection of rule-of-thumb techniques designed to get one's psychic talents to do more or less what one wants, more often than not, one hopes.

So what does "religion" mean? Here are my favorite definitions:

1. The body of institutionalized expressions of sacred beliefs, observances, and practices found within a given cultural context.

2. A magical system combined with a philosophical and ethical system, usually oriented toward spiritual beings.

3. A psychic structure composed of the shared beliefs, experiences, and related habits of all members (not just the theologians) of any group calling itself "a religion."

Now, what's a "ritual"? Again, there are many ways to define the term, but here is the one that I have found most useful:

> Any ordered sequence of events, actions, and/or directed thoughts, especially one that is repeated in the "same" manner each time, that is designed to produce a predictable altered state of consciousness within which certain magical or religious (or artistic or scientific?) results may be obtained.

One useful way to look at magic and the rituals associated with it is to consider the motivations of the people involved on a "secular-to-sacred" spectrum. Some see magic as a way to attain spiritual, intellectual, or psychological growth—this approach is known as "theurgy" (from Greek roots meaning "divine work"), and would include efforts to attain divine blessings, overcome an addiction or obsession, and so forth. Others do magic to change the physical world for the benefit of themselves and their loved ones—this approach is known as "thaumaturgy" (from the Greek for "wonder working"), and would include rainmaking, healing, blessing hunters with luck, and so on. Most Pagans (Paleo-, Meso-, and Neo-) have been or are interested in both. Thaumaturgy and theurgy are not opposites in a *dualistic* sense, but can be seen as one possible set of *polar* opposites, with an infinite number of possible steps in between. The vast majority of magical or religious rituals have a mix of the thaumaturgic and the theurgic.

With all that out of the way, let's look at the various sorts of magical and religious rituals that exist, all of which are done by some Wiccans on different occasions.

Most Wiccans tend to describe their rituals as being initiations, "sabbats" (holy day celebrations that are primarily theurgical), or "esbats" (monthly "working" rituals that are mostly thaumaturgical). Gerald Gardner took the second and third terms from the writings of the Renaissance witch-hunters. There are, however, more useful terms.

"Rites of worship" are mostly theurgical ones in which the primary purpose is to honor the Goddess and the God and to give Them our love and psychic (in both senses) energy. When done for more than the typically small coven, these rites become "liturgies" ("public works").

"Rites of passage" are ones in which the primary purpose is to recognize and/or cause a significant change in status/being of a new or current member of the religion. While this includes initiations, it also includes baby-naming ceremonies, coming of age rites, weddings, funerals, and so on. Wiccan initiations generally combine all three of the "types of initiation" that I have written about elsewhere: (1) recognition of status already gained, (2) ordeals of transformation, and (3) the "transmission of the gnosis" (psychically connecting the initiates with the wisdom of their predecessors).

"Rites of intensification" celebrate solar and lunar cycles, and thus "holidays," but may also serve to mark the beginning or ending of particular activities such as hunting seasons, planting and harvesting, and so on.

"Rites of passion" are ceremonies of a sexual nature, in which sex may be used for magical, psychic, and/or spiritual purposes or vice (you should pardon the expression) versa. These rituals are notable far more for their absence than their presence, as the vast majority of Neopagans are white, middle class, and still recovering from our dysfunctional childhood programming as antisexual Christians or Jews—not to mention our being surrounded by a sexually schizophrenic mainstream culture that can be guaranteed to misinterpret *any* sexual ritual.

"Rites of intimacy" are rituals done by couples or families, focused around the home and hearth, sometimes involving household shrines to matron and/or patron deities.

"Rites of solitude" are those rites done by individuals who have no others with whom they can share the other forms of ritual. While "solitaries" may no longer be the majority of Wiccans, they are still a large percentage of us.

"Rites of magic" are ceremonies done primarily to accomplish specific magical goals, usually thaumaturgical—today these might be job-hunting spells, attraction spells, healing spells, and so on. These are actually rarer than the image of the Witch as primarily a magic user would indicate.

It's possible, and indeed common, for two, three, or more of these types of ritual to be combined, depending on the talents, intentions, situation, and wisdom (or lack of it) of the parties involved. Sexual rites, for example, would not be combined with any other sort of ceremony at which children would be present or at which the general public is expected to attend. Solitary rites of passage can be difficult to pull off successfully, and all Wiccans may not recognize the results. Rites of intensification are usually combined with public rites of worship but may be solitary or familial events. Rites of worship may be combined with rites of magic when a community is faced with problems requiring divine assistance with spell-casting.

In the chapters that follow, I'll be focusing on rites of worship, with notes on combining these with the other sorts, for the simple reason that most Wiccan rituals involve worshiping the Goddess and/or the God regardless of whether or not other activities may also take place.

CHAPTER 14

# The Sources of Wiccan Ritual

egardless of the conflicting historical claims about whether there was ever a "real" coven into which Gerald Gardner was initiated, it is very clear from his own notes that he could have created the root liturgy of what was to become known as Wicca from available published sources and his own experiences in other Western occult organizations (books from several of which are known to have been in his personal library). I have studied the first draft materials found in Gardner's *Ye Bok of Ye Art Magical* (see chapter 9), which he eventually developed into the first *Book of Shadows*. There is simply nothing within its pages that can be demonstrated to be a remnant of a surviving underground British Paleo- or even Mesopagan religion prior to the 1800s.

There is a saying among scholars, "Absence of evidence is not evidence of absence," and generally this is true. However, in the field of liturgical design, missing evidence becomes quite important. *People writing rituals almost always start by reworking ceremonial materials with which they are already familiar.* As one example, the liturgies of the Episcopal and Lutheran churches resemble those of the Roman Catholic Church from which they sprung. For another, the rituals that Aleister Crowley wrote for his branch of the Ordo Templi Orientis—an offshoot of the Masons that he turned into a more magically "oriented" group—incorporate phrases and actions found in the older rituals of the Masons, the Hermetic Order of the Golden

Dawn, and the initiation rites of the pre-Crowlean O.T.O. For a third example (which, of course, "proves all"), most of the early rituals of the Druid organization I founded, *Ár nDraíocht Féin:* A Druid Fellowship (A.D.F.), included segments from the Reformed Druids of North America (R.D.N.A.) rituals I had learned years before; some of them, at least as I perform them, still do.

The earliest versions of Gardner's initiatory and liturgical scripts, as written by him in *Ye Bok*, are filled with obvious borrowings from Freemasonry, the Renaissance "Goetic" grimoires (magical books), the writings of Crowley, and so on. There are no prayers, incantations, ritual actions, or liturgical patterns that reflect any sources other than the (Judeo-Christian) Western mainstream of occult tradition, the then-available published materials on anthropology and folklore, some tantric sex-magical methods he could easily have picked up in the Far East or through Crowley, and some poetry lifted from Rudyard Kipling and William Butler Yeats, and other well-known poets. If Gardner had attended rites with genuinely Paleopagan elements in England, even if he were forbidden to put secret words and phrases down on paper, Paleopagan—or at least medieval Mesopagan—patterns of worship should be visible in his private notes.

However, except for some of the quotes from Mesopagan grimoires—which referred to ancient goddesses such as Astarte as male "demons"—none of his notes do. It has been suggested to me that the materials Gardner quoted from could themselves have contained legitimate Paleopagan fragments of "the Old Religion's" beliefs and practices, and that he just used the quotes he did because he liked the way these Mesopagan sources phrased things. This is about as unprovable and implausible as suggesting that these Mesopagan sources (the grimoires, the Christian translations of ancient Greek and Roman literature, the writings of Romance Era poets, Leland's *Aradia.* etc.) were telepathically inspired back through time from Gardner's writings in the mid-twentieth century. The technical term for this in modern logic is "grasping at straws."

The authenticity of Gardner's "apostolic succession" from a Secret

Underground Coven, whether going back to prechristian or late medieval times, therefore becomes irrelevant. If there *was* a "real" coven
(however defined) that trained Gardner, the members of it apparently
didn't show or tell him much of anything liturgical that was genuinely ancient or Pagan. This, however, may not matter much.

Gardner was extremely creative. He changed the goetic magical
techniques to make them usable by small groups of people instead of
solitary magicians. He rewrote the first three Masonic initiations to
make them applicable to both men and women (or stole them from
the Co-Masons). He made sensuality and eroticism a central part (at
least in theory) of his new/old religion by borrowing tantric techniques and symbolism. Finally, and most important, early in the
1950s he added Dion Fortune's syncretic* theology of Isis and Osiris
("All gods are one God and all goddesses are one Goddess") and other
polytheistic elements to make his creation genuinely Pagan—albeit
Mesopagan (he still had attitudes from his Christian upbringing in-
fluencing him subconsciously). Around 1954, all the notes he had
made during the 1940s and early 1950s were transferred to a new
book that became the first official *Book of Shadows,* and *Ye Bok* was retired to the back of a file cabinet, where it would lie forgotten for
twenty years.

Whatever their origins, the first versions of the Wiccan rituals in
*Ye Bok* (especially those for the holidays) were extremely sparse, being
usually only a page or two of text. Following Gardner's advice that "it
is ever better to do too much ritual than too little," the members of
his new religion added materials to them. Over the years, the rites
have expanded considerably, with enormous variations in detail but
with the same liturgical structure usually being more or less retained.

Of course, Gerald also wrote in his personal *BOS,* according to
Fred Lamond, "As you gain in experience you can gradually reduce
the amount of ritual and eventually drop it altogether. But newcomers

*"Syncretism" is the blending of many things, in this case deities, into one—in
this case, of each of two genders. This is also known as "theocrasy" (deity-blending)
by (poly)theologians.

must always be made to experience and practice the full rituals." Keeping the mid-twentieth century rituals intact and performing them for all newcomers to the Craft is part of what defines orthodox British Traditionalist Wiccans as such. After 50–60 years of performance, those rituals have gained some real magical power, despite how contrived or "silly" they might seem to outside critics. Nonetheless, the liturgical structures used by both these groups and other Wiccans can be seriously improved with a little experimentation and analysis, as I will do in the next chapter, which you are free to take with a few grains of consecrated salt.

# CHAPTER 15

# Current Variations in Wiccan Ritual Structure

or a variety of historical reasons, most of them having to do with (1) the secrecy of which Wiccans are so fond, (2) the seemingly constant necessity to invent new variations to convince students that one is not really stealing Gerald Gardner's and Doreen Valiente's material, and (3) Wicca's evolution as a typically decentralized postmodern collection of faiths, *there is no universal pattern for Wiccan ritual,* although the general shape is similar from group to group. Different Traditions do more or less the same ritual things but in differing orders and with different degrees of intensity and/or attention.

Most Traditions start with the participants doing some sort of personal purifications (herbal baths, fasting, etc.) before the ritual actually gets underway. These purifications are not prompted by a sense of impurity or sinfulness on the part of the participants, but reflect a need to begin focusing their consciousnesses, clearing away irrelevant thoughts, and showing respect for the Goddess and God, as well as for fellow coveners, much as members of many other religions do before attending services.

The nature of one's clothing (or lack of it) is another cue to one's inner self that sacred activities are about to take place, as well as another way to show respect to the Deities. Therefore, the people attending the ritual either dress in ceremonial robes or else strip down to a state of ritual nudity. The latter makes them "skyclad," from a Jain term applied to naked sages living in the woods who abandon all social concerns and class distinctions in their quests for enlightenment—another motive for Gardner to prefer it, in class-obsessed England.

Almost all Wiccan groups use a circle as the shape of their sacred space. Some have this shape physically marked on the ground or floor; most do not—which is why it often turns into a "magic oval." Most will have candles or torches set up, either just inside or just outside of the circle's line, at the North, South, East, and West sides of the circle. The spots are called "Quarter Points" or often just "the Quarters." Whether the directions are marked accurately with a compass or loosely as the room or other factors make convenient, also varies considerably.

Some Traditions have the almost universally used altar (usually a low table) outside this circle when the rite begins; others place it inside either at the center or near one of the Quarter Points.

Some groups have everyone except the presiding clergy (usually a High Priestess [HPS] and a High Priest [HP], sometimes also a Maiden and/or a Green Man as assistants) wait outside the ritual area, usually in the Northeast (for reasons having to do with Masonic initiations), while it is prepared for the ceremony, and bring them in afterward. Others begin with everyone in the circle.

Traditions that have the people in the circle and the altar outside of it may start with a "spiral dance" as first described by Gardner in *Witchcraft Today* and later in Starhawk's wildly influential *The Spiral Dance*. After everyone has spiraled into the center of the circle and spiraled out again, exchanging kisses along the way, and are once more standing in a circle holding hands, the ring will be broken and the altar brought in. Unfortunately, as all too many can testify, the spiral dance often turns into a spiral "crack the whip"—and no, I'm not referring to ritual scourging here! I usually don't recommend doing the spiral dance except to groups composed solely of young and healthy types dancing on a smooth, flat surface.

Salt and water are usually exorcised and/or blessed by the presiding clergy, sometimes along with other substances such as incense, oil, candles, and so on. These items are used, either before or after the circle is "cast" (symbolically formed) to exorcise and/or bless the circle as a whole and/or all the people in it. As with the personal purifications, exorcisms done in Neopagan rituals have little to do with banishing evil spirits and much to do with retuning the spiritual energies of the objects and/or persons involved to make them appropriate for the work at hand. Just as a cook who had been chopping garlic would take care to wash his or her hands and the knife before beginning to chop the apples for a pie—or at least we hope so—these ceremonial steps are taken.

The circle is cast, usually, by having the HPS or HP walk around it in a clockwise direction (except for some Wiccans in the Southern Hemisphere), starting at either the East Quarter Point (most common), the North (less common), or the South or West (both rare), with a consecrated sword, knife, wand, staff, or just fingers. These may be held in the air at any of several heights, pointed up, down, forward, or outward, or else dragged point-first along the floor or ground (the original technique in *Ye Bok*, where it was done by a male "Magus") along the desired circle boundaries.

The term "casting," by the way, used to mean "cutting" or "carving," which is why the Goetic magicians used sharp swords to actually mark the ground—and why I believe that a ceremonial Wiccan sword or knife should have a sharp point (edge, too, but that's another discussion).

Among some heterodox/Eclectic/fluffy/shallow Wiccans (choose your favorite adjective here), the circle is "cast" by everyone holding hands and declaring it cast, because having someone do it alone is "elitist." In public situations such as handfastings/weddings where many non-Wiccans are present, it can be cast by each person standing around the circle clasping the hand of the person to the left of them, who then does the same, all around the circle to the first person, while an appropriate chant* is repeatedly said.

*Such as, "The circle is cast from hand to hand, from heart to heart, from sea to land."

If the congregation waited outside the circle while it was cast, they will then be brought into it through a "gate" (usually in the Northeast if anyone is paying attention) either symbolically cut for them at that time, or left "open" during the casting process (and "closed" after their entry). People are brought into the cast circle in a formal fashion, generally with exchanges of passwords and/or kisses, often with aspergings, censings, annointings, and so on. Groups that practice binding and scourging (tying up one another with silk cords and gently "whipping" each other) may do it at this point in the ceremony, both as a purification process and as a way to start a flow of intentionally erotic *mana*,* or they may wait until after the "Quarter Point Invocations" (see below) have been done.

After the circle has been cast, exorcised, blessed, and so on, and the people are all present inside it (perhaps also exorcised and/or blessed), a series of invocations are usually spoken in four directions. These are done at or toward each of the previously mentioned Quarter Points, which are the points of the circle where two lines bisecting the circle at right angles, oriented to the East, South, West, and North, intersect it. These invocations may be to spirits variously addressed as "the Mighty Ones," "the Lords of the Watch Towers," "the totem animals," "the nature spirits," or sometimes to various gods and goddesses associated with the directions. Some groups will add an invocation to/from the center, and some to the nadir (ultimate bottom) and zenith (ultimate top) as well. All these invocations, by asking for the protection and cooperation of spiritual Gate Keepers, finish the process of creating sacred space by further defining the cosmos of the participants as one composed of the "Four Elements" plus Spirit, in which different directions partake of the nature of those elements.

In Starhawkian Wicca and some of the other heterodox Trads, the circle casting, Quarter Point Invocations, exorcism/blessing of the circle and people, and so on can be done completely or fragmentarily,

---

*Mana* is a useful Polynesian word that means magical, spiritual, artistic, emotional, athletic, and/or sexual energy. I haven't found another word yet that combines all these meanings so well.

and in any order or all at once, depending on the consensus and/or whims of the participants.

Once the circle is complete, there is often a ritual process of invocation or evocation known as "Drawing Down the Moon," which is usually done by the HP on behalf of the coven on the HPS (in a Feminist Wiccan circle the entire coven of women may speak the words). The intent is that the HPS (or sometimes all the women in the circle or everyone in the circle) will be able to manifest the Goddess to the coven through divine *inspiration, conversation, channeling,* or *possession.*

In this context, *inspiration* refers to the reception of ideas from the Goddess that arrive as abstract concepts without any pseudosensory input and that the HPS must then put into words of her own before passing them on. *Conversation* implies that she "hears" the Goddess's voice (sometimes accompanied by a vision of Her), can mentally converse with Her, and specific phrases can then be passed on from the Goddess. *Channeling* (also known as as "mediumship") means that the Goddess uses the HPS's vocal apparatus to speak directly with the others in what amounts to a light or "partial possession."

In all three of these levels of spirit communication, the HPS's awareness of her own spirit or soul is still in her physical body. In a total or "full possession," however, she will usually leave her body while the Goddess controls it and will often have no memory later of what her body was doing or saying while the deity was in it.

Sometimes, if she is sufficiently possessed by the invoked Goddess, the HPS may give the members of the congregation, individually or as a whole, pointed advice and information from the Goddess. More often, the HPS will deliver a memorized speech known as the "Charge of the Goddess." This has nothing to do with charging into battle or charging a bill to credit, but is from the Masonic habit of ceremonial officers giving "charges" (consisting of advice, expectations, and warnings) to their initiates. I suspect that the Charge was originally written so that an HPS who had failed to be literally (or literarily) inspired would have something worthwhile to say. Of course, being a good piece of prose—especially after Valiente rewrote it—the Charge is capable of being delivered in a truly electrifying manner that inspires new insights among the listeners.

A few Wiccan Traditions will then do "Drawing Down the Sun" on the HP (or again, sometimes on all the men or everyone in the circle). The HP may then deliver a "Charge of the Horned God" or other message from Him. Some Traditions might do the drawing down of the God before that of the Goddess at certain holidays and/or only during certain seasons of the year (when the Horned God is believed to rule the earth while the Triple Goddess sleeps). Many never do it.

Other forms of trance may be added to or substituted for Drawing Down the Moon and/or Sun. A ritual dance, more scourging, songs and chants, ritual dramas, initiations, handfastings (weddings) or other rites of passage, seasonal games, and/or spell-casting (in any combination and order) may follow or replace the Drawing(s) Down.

At some point, however, a ritual will be done that is known as "Cakes and Wine" (or "Cakes and Ale," "Cookies and Milk," etc.). This involves the blessing of food and drink by (usually) the HPS and the HP, then passing them around for the congregation to enjoy (the food and drink are passed around; hardly ever the clergy—darn it). Some Traditions offer libations to the ground when outdoors or in a bowl when indoors, before consuming the food and drink (libations made indoors are poured out onto the ground outdoors later).

Whether this communal meal is done before or after a rite of passage is performed or a spell is cast, and whether the meal is accompanied by general or topical discussion (if any), depends on a given group's theory of the meal's function. Some believe it's for strengthening the coven members before doing magic and/or filling them with energy from the God and Goddess; others that it's for relaxing and reviving after magic has been done. Some fulfill all these functions by passing the cup only around the circle, to fill the participants with the power of the Goddess and God, then doing their "working," then passing the cup around again with the cakes for revival and discussion/teaching.

Along with or (usually) as part of the Cakes and Wine ceremony is a magical act known as the "Great Rite." This is the primary symbol of the Sacred Marriage between the Goddess and the God, a central concept in Wiccan duotheology. The Great Rite was originally (in Gardner's notes) ritual sexual intercourse between the HPS and HP— or sometimes by all the couples in the coven—done to raise magical power, bless objects, and so on.

Nobody is saying whether Gardner ever performed the Great Rite (or what his wife might have thought of this); however, it's clear that almost from the beginning of Wicca, it has most often been done symbolically ("in token," as Gardner called it) rather than physically ("in true"), through plunging a dagger or wand into a cup to bless the wine or ale. Gardner was, after all, working with middle-class and working-class British occultists, not the lower-class or upper-class types who might have been less inhibited in their sexuality. The relaxed and healthy eroticism of the Paleopagans of ancient India or Britain was already long vanished, thus dooming his dream of a revived Western Tantra from the start.

The few American Wiccans of the 1970s who attempted to restore this aspect of the religion were denounced as sexist, exploitative, and politically incorrect by many in the Neopagan community and effectively silenced or cast out. As a result, the community lost any ability it might have had to establish appropriate ethical controls for such practices.

Occasionally, the Great Rite is used as part of a spell-casting or initiation or to consummate a handfasting/wedding. A handful of Traditions insist that some or all these purposes require the sexual act to be physical rather than symbolic, but even these few traditions usually remove the acting couple from the sight of the rest of the coven (or vice versa).

When the participants are ready to end their ceremony, the Goddess and/or the God, as well as the entities invoked at the Quarter Points, will be thanked and/or "dismissed." In some Traditions, excess *mana* will be "grounded" (drained). These steps are done in varying order. At the end, the circle is often cut across with a knife or sword, and/or the HPS walks quickly around it counterclockwise, and the ceremony is declared to be over.

There is confusion in the Wiccan Traditions and literature over the use of the terms "open" and "closed" when referring to the magical state of the circle. Some groups will say "the circle is closed" early in the rite to indicate that the magical barriers have been fully erected (after casting and exorcism/ blessing, etc.) and that therefore no one is to enter or leave without special permission and precautions (ritual "gate" making). Others will say, "the circle is closed" at the end of the rite, to mean that the ceremony has come to a close. Conversely, some Traditions say "the circle is open" early in the ritual in the sense of being "open for work" or the Gates between the worlds being open for communication with the Other Side. Still other groups will say "the circle is open" to mean that the ceremony is over and the magical barriers have been taken down.

This conflicting use of terms can be very confusing until you find out how a given group functions. Originally, the circle was opened at the beginning and closed at the end, following the Masonic practice of "opening" and "closing" lodge ceremonies (whence Gardner took the terminology).

All these variations in Wiccan ceremonial patterns fit roughly within what I call the "Common Worship Pattern" found in Indo-European religions.* Some Trads match it more closely than others. It has been my experience that Wiccan ritual can be far more powerful and effective, both thaumaturgically and theurgically, if a liturgical design is chosen that is as close a match as possible to the Common Worship Pattern. This can be accomplished most easily by adding the missing steps from that pattern.

One thing you might notice if you attend many Wiccan rituals is that they tend to be "top heavy": half to two-thirds of their ritual structure consists of setting up the sacred space and doing the preliminary power raising (calling the Guardians of the Quarters, etc.). The

*See my *Rites of Worship*.

supposed purpose for the rituals, the Drawing(s) Down and spell-casting or rites of passage, then take much less time, and the unwinding of the liturgy is often positively zoomed through. Perhaps these rites would be less top heavy if extensive trance, dancing, or other *mana*-generating and -focusing methods were used for spell-casting and/or rites of passage, instead of the five minutes' worth common in current Wiccan rites.

However, Gardner may have reasoned that modern Westerners need more time and effort to escape mundane reality than folks from other times and places did, so he deliberately elaborated the opening parts of the liturgy. Be that as it may, the ritual design presented next both inserts the "missing" parts of the Common Worship Pattern and makes the middle of the ritual more important than the beginning or end.

What follows on pages 128–29 is my expansion and ordering of the steps for a "standard" sort of Wiccan ritual—standard in the sense that you can be fairly sure this will regularly work as a ritual, not in the sense of it being required by anyone (including myself). I have done Wiccan ceremonies this way for decades now, with great success, and this is the pattern I teach my own Wiccan students.

As the reader will notice, the ritual is divided into five "phases" plus some preliminary and following activities. The lettered or numbered items in the outline are the observable steps of the rite as it is performed, while those items without letters or numbers are explanatory.

Because Wiccans may or may not wish to follow particular practices in a given Tradition, or on a specific occasion, optional activities and supplies are in italics, to make their status clear.

For those who may not be familiar with some of the terminology in the outline, here are some quick definitions:

"Briefing" means short instructions given to the participants before the ritual begins, about such matters as the name of the Goddess(es) and God(s) to be invoked, the words to any new chants to be used, any etiquette details that those new to a Wiccan circle might need to know, such as always walking clockwise in the circle or never crossing the boundary without special acts being done, etc.

"Clear-cut Beginning: Consecration of Time" refers to the actions taken to announce to all participants that the formal part of the ritual is beginning—in other words that sacred time is now commencing, as it must to begin any religious or magical ritual.* These actions may be as simple as ringing a bell, lighting a candle on the altar, or chanting "Aum."

"Blessing/Exorcism" means to clean and purify the altar, people, and the circle as a whole from inappropriate energies/feelings. Those of a more conservative orthodox persuasion will be likely to use the term "exorcism," due to the ceremonial magical tradition of always exorcising supposedly evil spirits that might have snuck into the magicians' equipment when he wasn't looking.

"Centering, Grounding, Linking, and Merging" refer to the process of creating the ceremony's group mind. This begins with everyone paying individual attention to their spiritual centers, wherever they may perceive them as residing in their body. Next, each participant feels his or her connection to the physical body and universe, often described as psychic roots growing into the ground below them. Next, the participants perceive/create psychic links connecting all of them. Finally, all merge into a group consciousness that exists underneath their individual identities.

The "Clear-cut Ending: Deconsecration of Time" obviously refers to the opposite of the corresponding step at the beginning, so that all the ritual's participants are returned to normal space and time. It's usually done by mirroring the actions taken before.

The meaning of the rest of the terms should be clear from the discussion earlier in this chapter.

---

*See *The Sacred and the Profane* and other works by Mircea Eliade for details on this concept.

# A Standard Wiccan Rite
*(Italics = optional activities)*

## Preliminary Activities
(A)   Briefing
(B)   Individual Meditations and Prayers
(C)   Sacred baths, other personal cleansing
(D)   Setting up the altar and ritual area
(E)   Ritual robing or disrobing

## Phase 1: Starting the Rite; Establishing the Group-Mind
Clear-cut Beginning: Consecration of Time
(1)   Announcement of Beginning
Consecration of Space and Participants
(2)   Blessing of the Elemental Tools
(3)   Casting of the Circle
(4)   Blessing/Exorcism of Altar, People, and Circle
Centering, Grounding, Linking, and Merging
(5)   Opening Unity Meditation
(6)   Ritual Purpose; Historical Precedent
(7)   Goddess *(and/or God)* of the Occasion; Reasons for Choice

## Phase 2: Re-creating the Cosmos; Preliminary Power Raising
Invoking the Gatekeepers; Defining the Circle as Center
(8)   Inviting the Guardians of the Quarters
(9)   "Between the Worlds" Chant/Affirmation

## Phase 3: Major Sending of Power to Goddess *(and/or God)*
(10)   Descriptive Invocation of Goddess *(and/or God)*
Primary Power Raising (a.k.a. "Cone of Power")
(11)   Participants generate mana (psychic energy) by dancing, singing, chanting, etc.
The Sacrifice/Gift of Mana
(12)   Releasing of energy raised (a.k.a. the "Drop")

## Phase 4: Receiving and Using Returned Power
Preparation for the Return
(13)   Meditation on Personal and Group Needs
(14)   Induction of Receptivity
Reception of Power from the Goddess *(and/or God)*
(15)   Drawing Down the Moon

(16)  Instruction from the Goddess; the Charge
(17)  *Drawing Down the Sun*
(18)  *Instruction from the God; the Charge*
(19)  *The Great Rite (or in Step 23)*
(20)  Cakes and Wine (Blessing and Passing)
(21)  Acceptance of Individual Blessings
Use of the Power Received
(22)  Reinforcement of Group Bonding
(23)  *Spell-Casting or Rite of Passage*
(24)  *Second Ritual Meal with Conversation and/or Instruction*

## Phase 5: Unwinding the Energies; Ending the Rite

Thanking of Entities Invited, in Reverse Order
(25)  Thanking the Goddess *(and/or God)*
(26)  Thanking the Guardians; Closing the Gates
(27)  Affirmation of Continuity and Success
Unmerging, Unlinking, Regrounding, and Recentering
(28)  Closing Meditation
Draining off Excess Mana
(29)  Charging of Tools *(or Giving to Earth)*
Deconsecration of Space
(30)  Circle Closing/Ending
Clear-cut Ending: Deconsecration of Time
(31)  Announcement of End (a.k.a. "Merry Meet and Merry Part")

## Following Activities

(F)  Hugs all around!
(G)  Return to secular clothing
(H)  Removal of libation bowl, etc., to outdoors

## Supplies List:

**Set:** table/altar, *fireproof cloth*, statues/images of Goddess *(and/or God)*, *Quarter Guardians/Elements symbols or icons*, Quarter candles/torches/lanterns, *cauldron, or other event-specific items.*

**Props:** *sword*, athame(s), boline, wand, pentacle, chalice, bowl, salt/soil dish, incense burner and incense and charcoal (or stick incense and holder), salt or soil, water, altar candles and holders, *crown for Goddess (and/or God)*, matches/lighter, plate, *cups for all*, cakes/cookies, *libation bowl*, wine/ale/ beer *(and/or juice/drinking water)*, napkins, bucket of sand or extinguisher, *broom, or other event-specific items.*

# CHAPTER 16

# A New Myth for Our Times

nce upon a time, when humans were first learning the rudiments of biological science and industrial technology, the Great Goddess, who is also known as Gaia, Danu, Nerthus, Oddudwa, the Earth Mother, and by many other names, saw that all Her children in the three worlds of the land, the waters, and the sky were in terrible danger. So She called unto Her mother, the Star Goddess, and unto Her children, the thousand gods and goddesses of earth, and cried out to them, "We must do something!"

"My mortal children are dying far before their time. The millions of years of evolution by which I created them and they created me are threatened by a crisis worse than any that have gone before. For the first time ever, one species among those to whom I gave intelligence are killing all the others—not just the ones they could eat or whom they feared, but even the ones they don't even know exist among the bacteria, the fungi, the plants, the insects, the birds, the reptiles, the fish, their fellow mammals—even ones the fools' own existence depends on!

"We must stop this, my mother, my children, or everything we have planned and nurtured for so very long will fail, you my immortal children will die for lack of worshipers, and I will have to start the long path over again with nothing but my one-celled children left."

Long did the Star Goddess, the Earth Mother, and the Old Goddesses and Gods confer until they had a plan.

"I shall appear as the white moon among the stars," said the Star Goddess, "and as the dark night reaching over all the world, and will speak unto the souls of mortal women and men, calling them back to my worship."

"I will call out unto my druids," said the Earth Mother, "as well as my godis, my flamens, and my mambos, calling them back to my worship and charging them to take action in the world of mortals to sound the alarms before it is too late."

"We, too, sleepy as some of us may be, will call new priests and priestesses," said the Old Deities, "to join those of our Sisters and Brothers who are awake, to infuse our worship with new energy and love, so we all may return to our former power and even greater wisdom."

Then spoke the Oldest of the Old, the bright shining flames of inspiration and the cool waves of deepest wisdom, They who had first brought the two-leggeds to stand upright and to master fire and to learn to carry the life-giving waters from place to place. "We, too, will call, to the poets, the musicians, the painters, the creators of arts as yet unknown, as well as to the scientists, the philosophers, and the wisest of the wise, that they may hear all your words and believe in their deepest hearts what they understand of your truths."

"Will it be enough?" asked the Earth Mother.

"Only time will tell, my daughter," said the Star Goddess, "but I have had to do this before, and will do so again for many of my other daughters, before time itself comes to an end, and every spirit in existence becomes One and starts over. Trust yourself, that you have fulfilled your destiny correctly, and that some of your children will hear our voices."

And lo—among those who walked on the earth, mortal men and mortal women lifted up their heads. And some of them heard.

So it was, so it is, and so it shall ever be.

This is how and why Wicca, and the rest of the Pagan revivals going on around the globe, began—with "dreamers and scholars, poets and rakes." They, like us, heard what the planet was trying to tell us. The old Myth of Wicca served its purpose, it got lots of people enthused (literally). But like the beloved fairy stories of our childhoods, it's time to put it on the shelf and create new myths to guide us into the future.

We who worship old deities should be willing to consider that the Goddesses and Gods *want* to be worshiped and therefore may have inspired countless small sects of people to revive what they thought the Old Religions (plural) were all about. These could have bubbled up over and over again, some lasting for decades and some for centuries, before attracting the attentions of the Church and the State. It isn't necessary for us to have, or our predecessors to have had, *unbroken* connections to the Paleopagan past, when the deities themselves can create those connections in the minds of their worshipers. Nonetheless, modern witches (of any variety) will be best served by using accurate history and avoiding grandiose, unverifiable claims.

What Wicca will become in the next few decades will depend on what the myriads of new Wiccans hear the Goddess saying to them in the depths of their hearts; on whether the "invading hordes" of teen Witches are willing to listen to the real wisdom of their elders in the Craft while forgiving our occasional nonsense; and on whether those elders are willing to open their circles to the influx of enthusiastic "kids" who may have more energy than sense, but who love the Goddess as much as we do.

I believe that Neopaganism in general, and Wicca in particular, are just beginning a period of fabulous growth and influence. So we'd better do it right (and rite!) making sure to keep this a healthy and sane alternative to the dinosaurs of dualistic dogma dying all around us. How can we safely do this without losing our way in the woods? The Goddess already told us how:

𝕷et my worship be within the heart that rejoices; for behold, all acts of love and pleasure are my rituals.

𝕬nd therefore, let there be beauty and strength, power and compassion, honor and humility, mirth and reverence within you.

So mote it be.

# WICCAN
# RESOURCES
# AND
# REFERENCES

# Etymological Notes

inguistic clues must be treated cautiously, since words are slippery, slithery things. Often the same word will be used for different concepts that are not always closely connected, and most languages have concepts that are referred to by several different words, depending on the emphasis desired. Even within a single tongue, both the spellings and the meanings of words change drastically with time. New words are invented and old ones forgotten; war and trade bring in slang and loan words that can replace venerable and respected terms. In addition, whenever possible we must consider the social and cultural environment in which a given word was used, a difficult task when most of the relevant data has been lost or destroyed.

We must also remember that ancient peoples did not know that linguists of later centuries would be trying to fit their word usage into nice, neat theories, so then as now they invented their own explanations for word origins, a process known to academics as "folk etymology." Since things can often become what they are called, we may observe the truth of the classic phrase that "ontology recapitulates philology."

English, German, Icelandic, Irish, Latin, Welsh, and several other tongues are all members of what linguists call the Western branch of the Indo-European languages. That branch, in turn, is one of several outgrowths of an original postulated mother tongue called Proto-Indo-European (PIE). By comparing variations of a word, not just within a given language, but among and between its sister tongues as well, it is often possible to trace back its linguistic development from an original (postulated) PIE root. Such roots are usually printed with an asterisk preceding them to indicate postulated forms, as in *weg- or *wy-.

Let's work backwards from Modern English. There are three nouns and two verbs in Modern English, all spelled "witch." The first noun comes from the Old English *wićća* (male), *wićće* (female), and *wiććan* (plural); probably all of these source words were pronounced with a hard "ch" sound as in "child" and/or with the "ch" said the same way the British say the "t" in "tune" (and that explains where the "t" in "witch" comes from).

This first witch noun has three meanings, according to the *Shorter Oxford English Dictionary (SOED, 5th Edition),* *the first of which is:

> A person, especially a woman, who practices magic or sorcery. Later also specifically (a) a person supposed or professing to have dealings with evil spirits and to be able to perform supernatural acts with their help; (b) a follower or practitioner of the religious cult of modern witchcraft, a Wiccan. OLD ENGLISH. **b** An ugly, repulsive, or malevolent (usually old) woman; a hag. LATE MIDDLE ENGLISH. **c** A fascinating, bewitching girl or young woman. MID-18TH CENTURY.

The second meaning of this first "witch" noun is obsolete; it used to be used as a synonym to "nightmare." The third meaning is that of various animals associated with or reminiscent of witches, as in "the stormy petrel" bird; or else a "dobby," which is "a mechanism attached to a loom for weaving small devices similar to but simpler than those produced by a Jacquard loom." Other meanings of "dobby" relate to house-brownies, as in the character depicted in J. K. Rowling's *Harry Potter and the Chamber of Secrets.*

The second "witch" noun comes from the Old English *wiće* or *wić,* apparently from the Germanic base to the word that became the

---

*This should be consulted for more details than the following discussion can include.

adjective "weak." This, the *SOED* tells us, is "a vague or general name for any of various trees having pliant branches; especially the mountain ash, *Pyrus aucuparia.*" As we will see, this is the connection to tree names such as "wych elm."

The third "witch" noun means a type of flatfish or flounder!

The first "witch" verb, on the other hand, comes from the Old English *wiććian,* apparently meaning whatever it is that witches do. There seems to be some connection to Middle and modern Low German *wikken, wicken,* which are of unknown origin. In later senses of the word, it probably came from people dropping the "be-" from "bewitch." As an intransitive verb, it means to "practice magic arts or witchcraft, use sorcery." As a transitive verb, it can mean to "affect or change (a person etc.) by witchcraft or sorcery; put a spell on." Both these verb forms can be used figuratively, usually when describing the effects that a "bewitching beauty" can have on her targets. "Witched" as an adjective probably comes from this first "witch" verb and can mean "bewitched, under a magic spell" or "possessed of magic power."

The second "witch" verb refers to dowsing, as in "water witching" and probably comes from the second noun version, since pliable branches are used for this purpose. Someone doing this is called a "witcher."

So "witchcraft" comes from the first "witch" noun plus "craft," and is the modern term for the Old English *wiććian,* in this case stressing the craft (as in "arts and crafts") aspect of spell casting or sorcery. It has its figurative uses too, as in many jazz standards wherein a male singer is claiming to have been bewitched by a fascinating (another occult term, meaning magically binding) woman or maid. It's no wonder that so many Feminist Witches suspect(ed) that the fear of witchcraft is primarily a fear of feminine power!

Another adjective of interest is "witchen" (rhymes with "bitchen"), a now mostly obsolete term referring to bent trees, as in "witchen elm."

Then there's another fascinating noun, "witchery." The "-ery" ending can mean "things of a certain kind," "a place of work," "a place

where things are bought," "a place where plants or animals are born
or reared," "a state or condition," "an occupation," or "characteristic
qualities, ideas or actions (often derogatory)," all of which could lead
to fruitful meditation when combined with "witch." "Witcheries"
was used during the persecutions of the imaginary diabolic witches to
indicate acts or examples of witchcraft.

But where do all these words come from originally? Let's see what
*The Oxford Dictionary of English Etymology* has to say:

**Witch** wɪtʃ [that symbol means "ch"] female magician or wizard. Old
English *wiċċa*, feminine corresponding to *wiċċe* male magician, sorcerer,
(whence dialectic *witch*), related to *wiċċian* practice magic arts, corresponding to Middle Low German *wikken*, *wicken*, agent-noun *wicker*,
and noun of action *wikkerie*, the source of which is unknown; later senses
of the verb are those of BEWITCH, of which in modern use it is mainly as
an aphetic [syllable dropping] derivative, surviving especially in echoes of
*the verie witching time of night* (Shakespear). Hence **witch**craft. OLD
ENGLISH *wiċċecræft.*

**wych-elm**, **witch-elm** wɪtʃelm, witch hazel, *Ulmus Montana.* 17TH CEN-
TURY ("weech elm" Bacon). Earlier *witchen elm* (16TH CENTURY); formed
on *wych*, *witch*, Old English *wiċe*, *wiċ*, probably from German *\*wik-*
bend (see WEAK) + ELM.

**Wych hazel**, **witch hazel** applied to various trees with pliant branches
16TH CENTURY. See preceding, HAZEL.

**Weak** wīk not strong, feeble 13TH CENTURY; *obsolete* pliant, flexible 14TH
CENTURY. MIDDLE ENGLISH *wayke* adopted from OLD NORSE *veikr*
(*\*weikr*) equals OLD ENGLISH *wāc* weak, slothful, pliant, insignificant,
mean (MIDDLE ENGLISH *wōke*), Old Saxon *wēk*, Old High German *weih*
(Dutch *week*, German *weich*, soft) normal development of Germanic
*\*waikwaz*, formed on *\*waikw-* *\*wikw-* yield, give way.

Many of the Germanic roots that grew into *wicce* and *wych* may
have come from a Proto-Indo-European root *\*wy-*, referring to willows and elms. This source word then began to be used to refer to the
literal and metaphorical characteristics of those trees, the sorts of

things made from them, and the techniques, such as twisting, weaving, and so on, used to make those things. See *Proto-Indo-European Trees*, by Paul Freidrich, for some intriguing arguments that are not known to most Wiccan scholars. I believe that it is a logical inference that various words related to the concepts of bending, twisting, weaving, and magic grew out of these roots and, like the willows and wych-elms themselves, entwined themselves around each other in the common people's minds.

I should mention that the PIE roots *weid-* and *wid-* are supposed to be the sources for both "wit" and "wisdom" (along with many other words involving vision, guidance, and the law), so someone wanting to keep the false etymology that *wicca* meant "wise one" could have switched to the Germanic term *witan* ("wise man") to cover her tracks, thus creating the modern pseudo-Irish faith known as Witta.

What words were used during the Dark Ages, Middle Ages, and Renaissance to translate *wicce, wicca,* and *wiccacraeft* into other European languages and vice versa?

The Greeks used the term *pharmakos* (source of our Modern English words pharmacist, pharmacy, etc.) based on the word *pharmakon* "drug, poison, spell." This is the etymological source of the American preacher Billy Graham's (in)famous statement, "The word witchcraft comes from the same word as drug and I think that proves something." It certainly would, if the Anglo-Saxons had spoken Greek.

However, the Greek use of *pharmakos* for both "poisoner" and "spell-caster" apparently supplied the excuse for Bible translators many centuries later to translate the Hebrew word *kasgah*, "poisoner" as "witch" in Exodus 22:18, "Thou shalt not suffer a witch to live." This mistranslation was designed to curry favor with the witch-phobic King James, for whom the translators of the King James Version made it a point to insert the English word "witch" into every possible verse concerning magical or divinatory activities in competition with the approved religious rulers.

Later, the Greeks used *magissa*, the feminine of *mago*, "magician" (from the Persian priesthood called the *Magi*) to translate *wicce*. Latin authors and translators used *saga*, from *sagire*, "to perceive keenly," *praesagire*, "to presage or foretell," as well as *striga*, "a vampiric night owl" (remember, they were thinking in terms of witches as criminals), *maga*, "a female magician," and *venefica*, "a female poisoner or magician," and so on. The Italians used *strega*, and the Romanians used *striga*, both derivations from the Latin. The Italians also used *maliarda*, "an evil charmer," and *fattuchiera*, from the Latin *fatum*, "fate." The French used *magicienne/magicien*, "a female/male magician," and *sorciere/sorcier*, "a female/male sorcerer."

The latter is usually explained as coming from the Latin *sortilegus*, meaning one who does divination or magic by casting of lots (small sticks or stones with special meanings) but may come from *sourcier*, meaning "a water-well finder" or "water diviner" (there's that witching and water witching connection again). Germans, Danes, and others used words that translate as "magician," "wonderworker," "spell singer," "diviner," or "knowledgeable one," all usually in the female form.

While some of these terms may have been positive or neutral in their original connotations, many were always negative and only these hostile interpretations seem to have been remembered into the Middle Ages. And note that none of them are terms that mean "midwife," "healer" or "priest/ess."

APPENDIX 2

# A Micro-Glossary*

 hese terms appear quite a bit in this work, so the following pages may prove helpful to the reader unfamiliar with how the meanings of these words have evolved over the centuries, and how modern Pagans may tend to use them.

"Paganism" (past usage): The term "Pagan" comes originally from the Latin *paganus,* which appears to have had such meanings as "suburbanite," "villager," "country dweller," or "hick." The Roman army used it to refer to civilians (and we know how fond career military men are of civilians). Polytheistic as they were, the residents of Rome would never have referred to themselves as "pagans," and were quite annoyed later when the early Roman Christians used "pagan" to refer to everyone who preferred to worship pre-Christian divinities. Over the centuries, "pagan" became simply an insult, applied to the monotheistic followers of Islam by the Christians, and vice versa, and by the Protestants and Catholics toward each other, as it gradually gained the connotation of "a follower of a false religion."

By the beginning of the twentieth century, the word's primary meanings became a blend of "atheist, agnostic, hedonist, religionless," and so on (when referring to an educated, white, male, heterosexual, non-Celtic European) and "ignorant savage and/or pervert" (when referring to everyone else). In the early twentieth century, various far-right groups began using the term to refer to their fascist/ Nazi philosophies, and some Mesopagans still do.

*Some of this material is taken from my *Polytheological Dictionary for Neopagans.*

"Paganism" (current usage): Today, many people in the English-speaking world proudly call ourselves "Pagan" with a capital "P," and to most of us "Paganism" is a general term for polytheistic and/or nature-focused religions, old and new, with "Pagan" used as the adjective as well as the membership term. Like "witchcraft," however, it requires something in front in order to clarify exactly what sort of Paganism one is discussing—prefixes are what we've settled on.

"Paleo-," "Meso-," and "Neopaganism" were defined in the introduction, so I need not repeat that material here.

"Theology," "Thealogy," "Duotheology," or "Polytheology": Intellectual speculations concerning the nature of God (singular, male), Goddess (singular, female), "the God and the Goddess" (dual, as syntheses of all male deities and all female deities), or the Deities (plural, all genders), respectively, and His, Her, and/or Their relations to the world in general and humans in particular. These activities generally involve "rational" explanations of religious doctrines, practices, and beliefs. These explanations may or may not bear any connection to any religion as actually conceived and practiced by the majority of its members, or to any system of logic not rooted in the same assumptions.

"Monotheism": A style of religion in which the theologians (or thealogians) claim that there is only one deity (theirs, of course) and that all other spirits claiming (or claimed) to be deities are "actually" demons in disguise (or a patriarchal plot).

"Henotheism": A style of religion in which one deity (out of many) is considered to be the king or queen of the Gods and assumed to be the proper prime focus of attention. This is what Judaism was, before all the other deities beside Yahweh were demoted in status to "angels" or "demons."

"Duotheism": A style of religion in which there are two deities accepted by the duotheologians, usually of opposite gender; all other deities worshiped are considered to be "faces" or aspects of the two main figures.

"Polytheism": A style of religion in which the polytheologians claim that there are many deities, of varying power and nature, and many lesser spirits as well, all of whom are considered to be "real" and to be possibly worthy of respect and/or worship.

"Dualism": A religious doctrine that states that all the spiritual forces of the universe(s) are split into Good Guys and Bad Guys (white versus black, male versus female, straight versus gay, etc.) who are eternally at war with each other.

"Polarism": A religious doctrine that states that all the spiritual forces of the universe(s) are split into Guys and Gals (good, weird, horny, scary, whimsical, etc.) who are eternally in bed with each other.

# Classifying Witchcrafts

s with the words "artist," "doctor," "scientist," or "diviner," the word "witch" is almost meaningless without some sort of qualifying adjective in front of it. Here is a brief review, in alphabetical order, of the classification system I have created to distinguish the various European and American sorts of witches from one another. Note that several of these categories are capable of overlapping and/or of being mixed by living individuals.

## Anthropologic Witchcraft

Anything an anthropologist calls "witchcraft," usually referring to either or both of the following meanings:

1. The practices of independent (real or supposed) magic users who are suspected of at least sometimes using their magic outside of their society's accepted cultural norms

2. A perceived state, often involuntary, of being a monster who can curse people with the "evil eye"

*See* Criminal Witchcraft (below).

## Christian Witchcraft, a.k.a. Christo-Wicca

The beliefs and practices of those who mix Neoclassic Witchcraft (see below) and/or Neopagan Witchcraft (Wicca) with a liberal form of Christianity, thus creating new Mesopagan versions of Wicca. Those who do primarily the former are often believers that "witchcraft is a craft," not a religion. Those who do primarily the latter are looked at askance by most Wiccans, who are inclined to think of them as "heretics."

Naturally, all but the most liberal of Christians consider people doing any flavor whatsoever of witchcraft to be heretics, since Christian priests, preachers, and ministers are supposed to have a complete monopoly on all performances of magic.

## Classic Witchcraft, a.k.a. Cunning Craft

The practices of the people that many modern witches think were the original witches, but who are more properly known as the cunning men and women. These folk were seldom called "witches" (at least to their faces) and could have any or all the following in their bags of tricks: midwifery; healing with magic, herbs, and other folk remedies; providing abortions, love potions, and poisons; divination; and casting of curses and blessings. Classic Witches have continued to exist to this very day, in ever dwindling numbers, mostly in the remotest villages and among the Romany or other traveling peoples.

## Criminal Witchcraft

Witchcraft as originally conceived by those who used the term first: the suspected or real use of magic for negative purposes—in other words, magical malpractice. This is probably what the word "wicce" originally referred to, annoying as that may be to modern Wiccans, and is very similar to the way anthropologists define witchcraft.

## Diabolic Witchcraft

An imaginary cult of Devil worshipers invented by the medieval Church, used as the excuse for raping, torturing, and killing scores of thousands of women, children, and men. The cult was said to consist of people who worshiped the Christian Devil in exchange for magical powers they used to benefit themselves and harm others. I used to call this "Gothic Witchcraft."

## Dianic Witchcraft

1. A postulated medieval cult of Diana and/or Dianus worshipers (Margaret Murray's idea).

2. Term used by some henotheistic Neopagan Witches to refer to their concentration on the Goddess as more important than the God.

3. Term used by some Feminist Witches, especially those who are separatist, to describe their practices and beliefs.

## Eclectic Witchcraft

The beliefs and practices of those on the liberal/heterodox end of the Wiccan spectrum. See "Traditional Witchcraft."

## Ethnic Witchcraft

The practices of various non-English-speaking people who use magic, religion, and alternative healing methods in their own communities and who are called "witches" by English speakers who don't know any better.

## Family Tradition or "Fam-Trad" Witchcraft

The practices and beliefs of those who claim to belong to (or to have been taught by members of) families that supposedly were "underground" Paleo- or Mesopagans for several centuries in Europe and/or the Americas, using their wealth and power to stay alive and secret. The overwhelming majority of the people you will ever meet who claim to be Fam-Trad Witches are simply *lying*, or have been lied to by *their* teachers. Family Tradition Witchcraft is also sometimes called "Hereditary Witchcraft" or even "Genetic Witchcraft." These latter terms are used by those people who think they must claim a witch as an ancestor to be a witch today or who think that such ancestry "proves" them to be better witches than those without such ancestry.

## Fairy/Faery/Faërie Tradition Witchcraft

1. Any of several different (and sometimes conflicting) Traditions of Meso- and/or Neopagan Witchcraft started by the blind poet and "scoundrel guru" Victor Anderson (1917–2001) during the 1970s, '80s, and '90s. He mixed British and Celtic folklore about the fairies, Gardnerianism, Voodoo, Max Freedom Long's version of Hawaiian Huna, Tantra, Gypsy magic, Native American beliefs, and anything else he was thinking about at the time he was training the founders of each Tradition.

2. Varieties of Neopagan Witchcraft focused around homosexual, bisexual, and/or transexual images and magical methods rather than the heterosexual (and sometimes homophobic) ones used in most Wiccan Traditions.

3. Other sects of Neopagan Witchcraft focused around real or made-up fairy lore, often taken from romantic poems, plays, and novels about the fairies. In most of these Traditions, there is usually an assumption that the medieval assumed associations between fairies and witches were true, and that the fairies were "originally" the Paleopagan nature spirits and/or deities.

## Feminist Witchcraft

Several new monotheistic or henotheistic religions started since the early 1970s by women in the feminist community who belonged to the women's spirituality movement and/or who had contact with Neopagan Witches. It is partially an outgrowth of Neopagan Witchcraft, with male deities booted unceremoniously(!) out of the religion entirely, and partially a conglomeration of independent and eclectic do-it-yourself covens of spiritually inclined feminists. The religions usually involve worshiping only the syncretic Goddess (who is all goddesses) and using Her as a source of inspiration, magical power, and psychological growth. Their scholarship is often abysmal and men are usually not allowed to join or participate.

Note, many other varieties of Witches also consider themselves feminists or act like ones whether they use the term or not.

## Gardnerian Witchcraft

The originally Mesopagan source of what has now become Neopagan Witchcraft, founded by Gerald Gardner and his friends in the late 1940s and '50s, based on his alleged contacts with a surviving British coven of underground Pagan Witches. After he finished inventing, expanding, and/or reconstructing the rites, laws, and other materials, copies of his work were stolen by numerous others who then claimed Fam-Trad status and started new religions of their own. (See Ronald Hutton's *Triumph of the Moon* for most of the messy details or appendix 7 for an overview.) Though Gardnerians are sometimes called "the scourge of the Craft," together with the Alexandrians and members of some other British Traditions, most of them may be considered simply the orthodox branch of Neopagan Witchcraft.

## Goth Witchcraft

People in the "Goth" subculture who practice one or more varieties of Neoclassic, Neopagan, or sometimes Neodiabolic Witchcraft. Goth Wiccans tend to focus on "dark" gods and goddesses (meaning ones that rule such matters as death and the underworld) and try to look scary.

## Grandmotherly Witchcraft

Refers to the habit common among modern Witches of claiming to have been initiated at an early age by a mother or grandmother who belonged to a Fam-Trad but who is now conveniently dead, doesn't speak English, and/or is otherwise unavailable for questioning.

## Immigrant Tradition or "Imm-Trad" Witchcraft

Refers to the customs and beliefs of postulated Mesopagan peasants and Fam-Trad members who immigrated to the Americas and mingled their magical and religious customs with each other, the Native Americans, enslaved African Americans, and the previous immigrants. Examples of such Traditions might include the dozens of kinds of American Voodoo and Hoodoo,* Pennsylvania "hex" magic, and Appalachian magical lore. I don't use this term much anymore since most of these people seem to be just eclectic cunning folk, who don't seem to consider what they do to be mostly religious.

## Neoclassic Witchcraft

The current practices of those who are consciously or unconsciously duplicating some or many of the (real or assumed) activities of the Classic Witches/Cunning Folk and who call themselves (or are called by others) "witches."

## Neodiabolic Witchcraft

The beliefs and practices of *some* modern Satanists, who work very hard to be everything that the medieval Church and current fundamentalists say they should be. Some of them perform Black Masses, commit blasphemy and sacrilege toward Christian ideas and objects, hold (or long to hold) orgies, and so on. There is some *small* overlap with the "Goth" subculture of the 1980s, but most Goths are not Satanists.

---

*See *Voodoo and Afro-Caribbean Paganism* by Lilith Dorsey.

## Neopagan Witchcraft or Wicca

Many new duotheistic religions founded since the 1960s, most of which are variations of Gardnerian Witchcraft but some of which are independent inventions and/or reconstructions based on real or supposed Fam-Trads, Imm-Trads, literary creations, and so on—just like Gardner's! Most groups who call what they do "Wicca" are Neopagan Witches, though some of the more orthodox may be considered Mesopagan ones.

## Neoshamanic Witchcraft

1. The beliefs and practices of those modern persons who are attempting to rediscover, duplicate, and/or expand on the practices of (postulated) Shamanic Witches.

2. Neopagan Witchcraft done with feathers, drums, crystals, and other New Age additions of a vaguely shamanic flavor. Most use drums and chanting rather than drugs to achieve their desired trance states.

## Shamanic Witchcraft

1. Originally, the beliefs and practices of members of *postulated* independent belladonna/Moon Goddess cults throughout premedieval Europe, remnants of which *might* have survived into the Middle Ages.

2. Currently, Neoshamanic Witchcraft as done by those who do not use the Neo- prefix.

## Traditional Witchcraft

1. The beliefs and practices of those on the conservative/orthodox end of the Wiccan spectrum. *See* Eclectic Witchcraft (above).

2. An extremely vague and badly abused term used by Gardner's competitors, supposed Fam-Trads, and other folks trying to make their practices seem older and more authentic than Wicca.

## witchcraft-with-a-small-w

The beliefs and practices of those modern persons following one or more varieties of Neoclassic and/or Neopagan Witchcraft who refuse to admit it, usually while claiming to be Fam-Trad Witches.

## Witta

1. An imaginary form of Paleo- and Mesopagan Witchcraft, supposedly practiced in ancient and medieval Ireland, yet called by a Germanic term.

2. A modern blend of Anglo-Saxon/Germanic Reconstructionist Paganism with Wicca.

# Principles of Wiccan Belief

ADOPTED BY THE COUNCIL OF AMERICAN WITCHES,
APRIL 1974

*This is the document mentioned in chapter 9 as having been the first attempt to synthesize a common set of beliefs for American Wiccans. While the organization behind it lasted only a few years, this statement has served as a touchstone for many Wiccans ever since.*

e are not bound by traditions from other times and other cultures, and owe no allegiance to any person or power greater than the Divinity manifest through our own being. As American Witches, we welcome and respect all life-affirming teachings and traditions, and seek to learn from all and to share our learning. We do not wish to open ourselves to the destruction of Wicca by those on self-serving power trips, or to philosophies and practices contradictory to these principles. In seeking to exclude those whose ways are contradictory to ours, we do not want to deny participation with us to any who are sincerely interested in our knowledge and beliefs, regardless of race, color, sex, age, national or cultural origins, or sexual preference.

1. We practice rites to attune ourselves with the natural rhythm of life forces marked by the phases of the Moon and the seasonal quarters and cross-quarters.
2. We recognize that our intelligence gives us a unique responsibility toward our environment. We seek to live in harmony with nature,

in ecological balance offering fulfillment to life and consciousness within an evolutionary concept.

3. We acknowledge a depth of power far greater than is apparent to the average person. Because it is far greater than ordinary, it is sometimes called "supernatural," but we see it as lying within that which is naturally potential to all.

4. We conceive of the Creative Power in the Universe as manifesting through polarity—as masculine and feminine—and that this same creative Power lives in all people, and functions through the interaction of the masculine and feminine. We value neither above the other, knowing each to be supportive of the other. We value sexuality as pleasure, as the symbol and embodiment of Life, and as one of the sources of energies used in magickal practice and religious worship.

5. We recognize both outer worlds and inner, or psychological worlds—sometimes known as the Spiritual World, the Collective Unconscious, the Inner Planes, etc.—and we see in the interaction of these two dimensions the basis for paranormal phenomena and magickal exercises. We neglect neither dimension for the other, seeing both as necessary for our fulfillment.

6. We do not recognize any authoritarian hierarchy, but do honor those who teach, respect those who share their greater knowledge and wisdom, and acknowledge those who have courageously given of themselves in leadership.

7. We see religion, magick, and wisdom-in-living as being united in the way one views the world and lives within it—a world view and philosophy of life, which we identify as Witchcraft or the Wiccan Way.

8. Calling oneself a "Witch" does not make a Witch—but neither does heredity itself, or the collecting of titles, degrees, and initiations. A Witch seeks to control the forces within him/herself that make life possible in order to live wisely and well, without harm to others, and in harmony with nature.

9. We acknowledge that it is the affirmation and fulfillment of life, in a continuation of evolution and development of consciousness that

gives meaning to the Universe we know, and to our personal role within it.

10. Our only animosity toward Christianity, or toward any other religion or philosophy-of-life, is to the extent that its institutions have claimed to be "the one true right and only way" and have sought to deny freedom to others and to suppress other ways of religious practices and belief.

11. As American Witches, we are not threatened by debates on the history of the Craft, the origins of various terms, [or] the legitimacy of various aspects of different traditions. We are concerned with our present, and our future.

12. We do not accept the concept of "absolute evil," nor do we worship any entity known as "Satan" or "the Devil" as defined by Christian Tradition. We do not seek power through the suffering of others, nor do we accept the concept that personal benefits can only be derived by denial to another.

13. We work within nature for that which is contributory to our health and well-being.

## An Analysis

While Neopagan Witchcraft has no creeds that all must subscribe to, this document gives a good summation of what most Wiccans more or less agreed about as early as 1974 (compare it to my discussion in chapter 12). There were only about 75 or so people who participated in Weschke's Witchmeet, but I knew many more who weren't there but who would have agreed with those present, mostly because the vast majority of them were doing variations on basic Gardnerianism, at a time only a few years removed from Wicca's creation. I have seen efforts to dismiss these principles as worthless, unrepresentative, inaccurate "rules," since they don't all apply to every single person who might ever call him- or herself a Wiccan—let alone any other kind of witch. These objections gloss over some important philosophical issues.

First, this document was meant to be descriptive, not prescriptive. It was idealistically describing what this group of people said they believed and practiced, not what they thought other Wiccans *should* believe and practice—let alone including everybody past, present, or future who might ever call themselves "witches." All groups, including the short-lived Council of American Witches, have a right to describe themselves and what they do or do not believe, regardless of what outsiders or later generations might agree or disagree with in their statements.

Second, these principles turned out to be very accurate in describing how the majority of American Wiccans in the 1970s, '80s, and '90s viewed their religious beliefs. The fact that a small number of people today call themselves "witches-with-a-small-w" (in other words, non-Wiccan witches) yet still want to be part of the Neopagan community that is dominated by Wiccans, does not constitute a legitimate challenge to the principles, but raises questions of the critics' motives. If one is not a Wiccan, why would one care how Wiccans describe themselves?

Third, if most of the people belonging to a group agree on something, then a few others who want to call themselves members of the group have no right to tell the overwhelming majority that they can't define their group's beliefs, or that they have to accept everyone as members even if they disagree with several of the group's previously agreed-on beliefs. This is an extreme example of the American culture's obsession with individual freedom at the expense of a community's welfare. The preamble to these principles clearly states that the participants did not wish to open themselves "to the destruction of Wicca by those on self-serving power trips, or to philosophies and practices contradictory to these principles." That's a fair warning to contrarians.

Fourth, there have been criticisms that these principles are "too vague," that they don't cover every topic that Wiccans might consider important, and that they are easily nitpicked to death by anyone with an axe to grind. Consider, however, that this was a first group attempt to describe a new religious movement, during a gathering where many of the Council members were jealously guarding their "secrets" (mostly the secret that none of their Trads were as ancient as they claimed) and that some of the participants were only grudgingly co-operating in the project. It was a major act of magic that any kind of statement at all was produced of which the majority would approve. Of course, there are those who equate "witchcraft" with "magic" and want to have members of every magical system on the planet accepted as witches (at which point the term becomes useless), so they don't like the way the Principles were written because they make them feel excluded from the Club (excuse me, the Craft). Why do I find myself thinking that some folks just never got over high school?

The only solid objection I've heard to the principles was that they equated witchcraft with (mostly conservative orthodox) Wicca and, as this book has demonstrated, that's an equation that fails miserably. In 1974, however, one of the core Wiccan beliefs was that all previous witches had been underground Wiccans and that Satanists and other non-Wiccans couldn't be real Witches. The fact that we now know these to have been false assumptions does not require us to dump everything else in the document, it merely emphasizes that, like every other historical document, it must be examined in its historical context and not in an artificial isolation from the real lives being led by the people who composed it. In 1974 there was no widely accepted classification of different varieties of witchcraft (as in appendix 3), just a dualistic belief that one either was a "witch" or one wasn't.

For a while, I was confused about the origins of the principles, actually believing that I had written the first draft of them. Carl Weschke, however, tells me, "I wrote the Principles and proposed them for adoption. I worked on them into the wee hours of the night. I don't remember if they were adopted without change or not—it seems to me that there was one minor change. As far as I'm concerned, this was my greatest contribution to the movement." He might very well be right, because these Principles shaped the evolution of Wicca in America for decades afterward.

# Recommended Books on
# Ancient and Modern Witchcraft

he following books will get you *started* on understanding Paleopagan, Mesopagan, and Neopagan Witchcraft. This topic is so complex that choosing titles and categories is extremely difficult, so remember that these are my current recommendations, not a list of "officially approved texts."

## Magic, Witchcraft, and Religion in Paleopagan Europe

*The Destiny of a King, The Plight of a Sorcerer, The Stakes of the Warrior, Archaic Roman Religion, Mitra-Varuna,* and others by Georges Dumézil. All worth reading if you want to know what pre-Christian European Paganism was really like.

*Shamanism: Archaic Techniques of Ecstasy* by Mircea Eliade. This is the classic text on the topic, the one that made the term "shaman" well known before Carlos Castaneda, Michael Harner, and Lynne Andrews blurred it into uselessness. Why put it here? Because many modern Wiccans incorrectly believe that early witches were shamans. I also highly recommend his three-volume series *A History of Religious Ideas.*

*The Myth of Matriarchal Prehistory: Why an Invented Past Will Not Give Women a Future* by Cynthia Eller. The Goddess doesn't need us to tell lies for Her. Eller analyses all the bits of the Universal Golden Matriarchal Age mythology and shows where they came from and why we can't believe them. She doesn't seem to be aware, however, that even the die-hards have been backpedaling recently.

*Proto-Indo-European Trees* by Paul Freidrich. Primarily a linguistic monograph, this is the only book to cover in detail the various species of trees known to have had names in the PIE language. He includes a great deal of religious and symbolic detail without always realizing that he is doing so. The chapters on willows, elms, and oaks are most relevant for the history of witchcraft. Out of print but well worth hunting for.

*The Pagan Religions of the Ancient British Isles: Their Nature and Legacy* by Ronald Hutton. This is a brilliant review of the history, prehistory, and pseudohistory of British Paleopaganism.

New from Ronald Hutton! *Shamans: Siberian Spirituality and the Western Imagination*. This will be a good book to read after Eliade's *Shamanism*.

*A History of Pagan Europe* by Prudence Jones and Nigel Pennick. Not as scholarly as Hutton, yet certainly far better than the average work published on this topic. At least they don't include the common nonsense about universal matriarchies, unbroken lines of survival back to the Stone Age, and so on. Their Baltic and Scandinavian materials may be a little shaky, however.

*The New Comparative Mythology: An Anthropological Assessment of the Theories of Georges Dumézil* by C. Scott Littleton. This is the best critical introduction to Dumézil's work, with an extensive bibliography of relevant books and articles by Dumézil and others. While others (including myself) have enlarged on his theories, his views of common Indo-European cultural patterns (including religious beliefs, social classes, institutions, and practices) were essentially sound and deserve careful study.

*The New Book of Goddesses and Heroines* and *O Mother Sun: A New View of the Cosmic Feminine* by Patricia Monaghan. The first is a new edition of a classic work that is infinitely superior to many with similar titles. The second does an excellent job of showing that Sun Goddesses were just as common as Moon Goddesses to our Paleopagan ancestors. For many years, Monaghan was nearly alone as a feminist scholar who really is as committed to scholarship as she is to her feminism.

*Celtic Heritage: Ancient Tradition in Ireland and Wales* by Alwyn Rees and Brinley Rees. A classic Dumézilian analysis of Celtic mythology and religion, based primarily on Irish and secondarily on Welsh materials. Gives an excellent overview of basic patterns of belief, showing how they reflected the social structures of the Celts—and vice versa!—and will explain much of the cosmology underlying real Celtic mythology and ritual (see *Bonewits's Essential Guide to Druidism* for details).

If you're wondering why most of this category is focused on Britain, it's because that's where modern Neopagan Witchcraft came from as well as where it claimed its roots were.

## Mesopagan Witchcraft: The Hunts

*Witchcraze : A New History of the European Witch Hunts,* by Anne L. Barstow. The author goes a little overboard on her gender analysis, but is otherwise informative.

*Witches and Neighbors: The Social and Cultural Context of European Witchcraft* by Robin Briggs. This work provides the vital close-up view of how small town hostilities could erupt into witchcraft accusations.

*The Inquisition: The Hammer of Heresy* by Edward Burman. A historical overview of seven centuries of activity by the Unholy Office of the Inquisition. The author attempts to steer a middle path between various scholarly controversies. Remarkably, the "gentle" Franciscans get the blame they deserve, rather than just the Dominicans and Jesuits.

*Thinking with Demons: The Idea of Witchcraft in Early Modern Europe* by Stuart Clark. A detailed analysis of how Christian dualism promoted the ideas that eventually led to the great witch hunts.

*Europe's Inner Demons: The Demonization of Christians in Medieval Christendom* by Norman Cohn (revised edition). A classic work on the psychological and social origins of witch hunts. He covers the history of the ancient urban legend of baby eating and incestuous orgiasts revived by modern Christian fundamentalists.

*The Night Battles: Witchcraft and Agrarian Cults in the Sixteenth and Seventeenth Centuries* by Carlo Ginzburg. Yes, there really were people who thought they could fly through the air at night—only these folks did it to *fight* (what they thought were) witches. Then the Inquisition came along.

*Compendium Maleficarum* by Francesco Maria Guazzo. This was the early seventeenth-century successor to the *Malleus Maleficarum,* written by a man apparently just as gullible (or just as evil) as Heinrich Kramer and James Sprenger were.

*Witch Trials: Their Foundations in Popular and Learned Culture* by Richard Kieckhefer. How what the intelligensia believed and the peasants believed collided, merged, then separated again.

*Witchcraft in Europe, 400–1700: A Documentary History* by Alan Charles Kors and Edward Peters (editors). When you actually read the documents of the times, you get a very different picture from both what we were taught in school and the current tales some Neopagans tell.

*The Malleus Maleficarum* by Heinrich Kramer and James Sprenger (translated with introduction, bibliography, and notes by Montague Summers). This is an officially approved (the Papal *imprimatur* has never been rescinded) 1486 theological tome used by many inquisitors as "justification" for the atrocities committed against women, children, and men for the thought-crime of Diabolic Witchcraft. There are Christians today who still accept their arguments and "evidence" of Satanic wrongdoing (though many would be shocked to know they were agreeing with Roman Catholic theology). Summers was a "Gnostic Catholic" priest and occultist who wrote credulous tomes about werewolves and vampires and comments approvingly throughout his translation.

*The Witchcraft Sourcebook* by Brian Levack (editor). He has edited and written several academic works on witchcraft since 2000.

*The Encyclopedia of Witchcraft and Demonology* by Rossell Hope Robbins. Even though he is a total cynic on the subject of magic, his book is one of the standards on the subject of Diabolic Witchcraft and the Inquisition. He will tell you a great deal more than you really want to know about the torturing methods used against accused Diabolic Witches. His body counts, however, are untrustworthy.

*Witch Craze: Terror and Fantasy in Baroque Germany* by Lyndal Roper. This work focuses on a close examination of one geographical region.

*The Devil: Perceptions of Evil from Antiquity to Primitive Christianity, Satan: The Early Christian Tradition, Lucifer: The Devil in the Middle Ages, Mephistopheles: The Devil in the Modern World* by Jeffrey Burton Russell. The author traces the "history" of the Christian Devil in exhausting detail. If you're short on time, you might want to read his summating volume *The Prince of Darkness* instead.

*Witchcraft and Magic in Sixteenth and Seventeenth Century Europe* by Geoffrey Scarre and John Callow. A good summation of what scholars learned during the 1980s and '90s.

## Mesopagan Witchcraft:
## The Background of the "Revivals"

*The Golden Bough* by Sir James Frazer (I prefer the 3rd edition). One of the earliest and most influential works in the field of comparative mythology, at least as far as the English-speaking world was concerned. By the 1930s, most of his theories and interpretations were no longer accepted by social scientists, yet many of his core ideas became and remain a part, not just of Neopagan Witchcraft, but also of Western culture as a whole during the early part of the twentieth century.

*The White Goddess: A Historical Grammar of Poetic Myth* by Robert Graves. While the history, comparative mythology, and Celtic studies in this book are worthless, this book was one of the major sources of ideas for what was to become Mesopagan, then Neopagan Witchcraft. Unlike most of his other works, therefore, I can recommend it solely as an historical curiosity.

*Aradia: or, the Gospel of the Witches—Expanded Edition* by Charles

Leland, translated by Mario (and Mama) Pazzaglini. A fresh translation of one of Gardner's main sources, with commentary by modern writers, some of them scholarly and some of them not. Leland was a respected folklorist when he first published this work describing an underground Pagan cult in the mountains of Italy that had supposedly survived to his day (1899).

*The Witch-Cult in Western Europe*, *The God of the Witches*, and *The Divine King in England* by Margaret Murray. Almost everything she had to say about the supposed survivals of Paleopagan cults into the Middle Ages (when their supposed members were persecuted as witches) has been thoroughly disproved by modern scholarship. Yet, these are still important books with which modern Witches should become familiar.

## Mesopagan Witchcraft: The "Revivals" Themselves

*The Robert Cochrane Letters* by Robert Cochrane (edited by Evan John Jones, with Michael Howard). Cochrane taught many of his students via letters; this book collects many of them.

*A Goddess Arrives* and *High Magic's Aid* by Gerald Gardner. The first one is a (bad) novel, in which Gardner first explored ideas of reincarnation and Goddess worship. The second is another novel in which he reveals much of his thinking during the years he was first creating Wicca. Both are now available in reprint editions from the Church and School of Wicca at www.wicca.org and other online dealers.

*Witchcraft Today* and *The Meaning of Witchcraft* by Gerald Gardner. The (officially) non-fiction books in which he revealed to the world that a secret underground religion of Pagan Witchcraft had survived into the twentieth century, and what it was all about. Available in a special two-book package with a CD of Gardner being interviewed and reciting incantations, from Mercury Publishing at www.mercurypublishing.com and other online dealers.

*What Witches Do: The Modern Coven Revealed* by Stewart Farrar.

One of the first books published about the Alexandrian Tradition of Wicca, which at the time was 95 percent identical to Gardnerianism.

*Good Witch's Bible* by Gavin Frost and Yvonne Frost. Originally published as "*The*" *Witch's Bible*, it caused an uproar among American Wiccans because, among other crimes, it presented a form of Wicca that differed significantly from Gardner's. The authors claim that their form of Wicca comes from a British occult group that was competing with Gardner.

*Wiccan Roots: Gerald Gardner and the Modern Witchcraft Revival* by Philip Heselton. A complementary study to Hutton's *Triumph*.

*The Triumph of the Moon: A History of Modern Pagan Witchcraft* by Ronald Hutton. Tells how Wicca was created in the mid-twentieth century, based on literary, artistic, and academic fashions, the practices of fraternal orders and occult societies, old and new folk customs, and other cultural roots (real and imagined) going back to the 1700s. Hutton leaves no hope for those who wish to believe in a constantly existing Pagan religion in Britain or in a connection between the early modern witch trials and Paganism. *No one can claim to be knowledgeable about the true history of modern Witchcraft who has not read and carefully studied this text.*

*Witchcraft: A Tradition Renewed,* by Evan John Jones & Doreen Valiente. All she wrote was the Intro, but this is a good overview of Robert Cochrane's approach to inventing a Pagan Witchcraft.

*The Roebuck in the Thicket,* by Evan John Jones & Robert Cochrane (ed. by Mike Howard). More on Cochrane's system.

*Crafting the Art of Magic, Book I: A History of Modern Witchcraft, 1939–1964* by Aidan Kelly. This is an excellent work of textual criticism of the key Gardnerian materials, showing where every line was borrowed or invented. Unfortunately, a constant stream of essentially pointless cheap shots at Gardner's sexuality mars what should have turned into a classic of religious history.

*The Rebirth of Witchcraft* by Doreen Valiente. Her history of how she, Gardner, and a few friends created Wicca. Among other things, this is the book in which she finally took credit for her poetry and

prose that many had been blithely calling "traditional" (and then pla-
giarizing).


## Neopagan Witchcraft: The Beginnings

*Buckland's Book of Saxon Witchcraft* by Raymond Buckland. Originally published as *The Tree,* this is the book in which the author invented Seax-Wica, the first tradition of Wicca in which self-initiation
was explicitly approved.

*The Truth about Witchcraft* and *Wicca: A Guide for the Solitary
Practitioner* by Scott Cunningham. The first book is an excellent brief
introduction to general Wicca, suitable for giving to worried friends
and family. The second was the first widely distributed text on Wicca
aimed at readers who had no coven or prospects of having one. Very
controversial when first published, but now recognized as a classic.

*The Witches' Goddess: The Feminine Principle of Divinity, The
Witches' God: Lord of the Dance,* and *A Witches' Bible* by Janet Farrar
and Stuart Farrar. The first two books contain useful details about
multiple deities and how their worship can be incorporated into
Wiccan circles. The third is a rebinding of both *Eight Sabbats for
Witches* and *The Witches' Way,* so it's a good introduction to the early
orthodox Traditions of Wicca, with lots of fine ritual ideas.

*The Spiral Dance, Dreaming the Dark,* and *Truth or Dare* by Starhawk. Starhawk was the first writer to discuss the political and social
implications of Goddess worship in general and magic in particular.
Unfortunately, she backed off from her radicalism as she began to sell
to the New Age market.

*An ABC of Witchcraft Past and Present* and *Witchcraft for Tomorrow*
by Doreen Valiente. The first is a dictionary of sorts, used as a primary reference by many Wiccans during the 1980s and '90s. The second presents her thoughts near the end of her life about Gerald
Gardner, Wicca, and her role in the process of its creation (includes a
lovely "Book of Shadows" section with prayers and ritual instructions).

## Neopagan Witchcraft: Some Recent Worthy Titles

*Deepening Witchcraft: Advancing Skills and Knowledge* by Grey Cat. It's difficult to know what category to put this one in! An experienced Witch, Druid, and all-around troublemaker, Grey Cat provides a workbook/study guide/history for those Wiccan priests and priestesses ready to get serious about professionalism and competency in their Craft. When you don't know where to go to get the skills you need to serve your community, dig out this book, but be prepared— like my own writing, Grey Cat's is guaranteed to have something to offend nearly everybody!

*Wiccan Warrior: Walking a Spiritual Path in a Sometimes Hostile World* by Kerr Cuchulain. A Pagan cop talks about what being a "warrior" means to him.

*Living Wicca: A Further Guide for the Solitary Practitioner* by Scott Cunningham. A sequel to his *Wicca: A Guide for the Solitary Practitioner*, this takes the individual Wiccan deeper into the Craft.

*Book of Shadows: A Modern Woman's Journey into the Wisdom of Witchcraft and the Magic of the Goddess* by Phyllis Curott. The author was a high-powered corporate lawyer in New York City and a long-time member of the Covenant of the Goddess. Her book tells how she has managed to follow a spiritual path seemingly a few centuries and several thousand miles away from her secular life.

*The Way of Four* by Deborah Lipp. Meditations on the four elements and their role in Wiccan philosophy.

*The Goddess Path: Myths, Invocations and Rituals* by Patricia Monaghan. The author of *The New Book of Goddesses and Heroines* presents a beautiful guide to contacting twenty different goddesses within, from cultures around the world. This is a spiritual workbook with questions and activities to be answered and performed by the reader.

*To Ride a Silver Broomstick: New Generation Witchcraft, To Stir a Magick Cauldron: A Witch's Guide to Casting and Conjuring,* and *To Light a Sacred Flame: Practical Witchcraft for the Millennium* by Silver

RavenWolf. These books are among the clearest written for beginning and intermediate students of Wicca, although they do tend to be very "fluffy bunny" in their approach.

*When, Why . . . If* by Robin Wood. The famous fantasy and tarot artist provides an in-depth discussion of ethics from a Wiccan perspective. Readers may also enjoy her *Theory of Cat Gravity*, which explains many mystical matters that have long confused cat owners. Both books are available through her Web site at www.robinwood. com.

## Neopagan Witchcraft: Books for Pagan Parenting

*Celebrating the Great Mother: A Handbook of Earth-Honoring Activities for Parents and Children* by Cait Johnson and Maura D. Shaw. Great ideas for sharing your reverence for the Earth with your children.

*Pagan Kids' Activity Book* by Amber K. A coloring book for kids from four to eight, showing pictures of Pagan deities and worshipers.

*Pagan Parenting: Spiritual, Magical and Emotional Development of the Child* by Kristin Madden. Shows how even the simplest of activities can bring magic to a child's soul.

*The Family Wicca Book: The Craft for Parents and Children* by Ashleen O'Gaea. Down to earth advice on sharing the Wiccan religion with your children, parents, and other family members, whether you are an experienced or brand-new Wiccan. Also good by her: *Raising Witches: Teaching the Pagan Faith to Children.*

*Teen Witch: Wicca for a New Generation* by Silver RavenWolf. Rather than bemoaning the current flood of teenagers interested in the Craft, the author prefers to empower them! In this best-selling title, she tells teens—and their parents—what they want and need to know about Wicca.

*Circle Round: Raising Children in Goddess Traditions* by Starhawk, Diane Baker, and Anne Hill. Ways to teach children an Earth-centered spirituality using songs, stories, and simple rites.

## Neopagan Witchcraft: Academic & Journalistic Observations

*Drawing Down the Moon: Witches, Druids, Goddess-Worshippers, and Other Pagans in America Today,* 4th edition, by Margot Adler. This is the latest edition of the classic book about the Neopagan movement in America—a book that galvanized the very community it was describing and changed it forever. *Every member of the Neopagan, Wiccan, and/or Goddess Worship movements in the United States should own this book*—at least if he or she wants to understand our history since 1960.

*A Community of Witches: Contemporary Neo-Paganism and Witchcraft in the United States* by Helen A. Berger. A look at the evolution and growth of Wicca in the United States over the last three decades.

*Witchcraft and Paganism in Australia* by Lynne Hume. A scholar from down under describes the history of Australian Wicca and the ways in which it has adapted to a very non-European environment.

*Magical Religion and Modern Witchcraft* by James R. Lewis (editor). An anthology of essays by scholars, some of them within the Neopagan community, others complete outsiders.

*Persuasions of the Witch's Craft: Ritual Magic in Contemporary England* by T. M. Luhrman. An anthropologist's "participant observation" research into the structures, personalities, beliefs, relationships, and concerns in some British covens. Highly educational for anthropologists and other social scientists, especially about the ethical and emotional conflicts inherent in pretending to join a religious community.

*Never Again the Burning Times: Paganism Revived* by Loretta Orion. A sociological examination of U.S. Neopagans, built around a survey the author distributed at a number of Pagan festivals. Some interesting and intriguing insights into what makes Neopagans who and what we are.

## Neopagan Witchcraft: Holy Days

*Eight Sabbats for Witches* by Stewart Farrar. The first book published that attempted to provide not just ritual scripts but a rationale for the eight-holiday system Gardner and friends adopted—and it wasn't easy! Also available bound as part of *A Witches' Bible* with *The Witches' Way.*

*Stations of the Sun: A History of the Ritual Year in Britain* and *The Rise and Fall of Merry England: The Ritual Year 1400–1700* by Ronald Hutton. Like his other titles, these will shock and surprise those of us who thought we knew all about Pagan holidays.

*The Pagan Book of Days: A Guide to the Festivals, Traditions, and Sacred Days of the Year* by Nigel Pennick. Discusses mostly European holidays and explains the astronomical and seasonal origins of most of them.

## Neopagan Witchcraft: The Rite Stuff

*Real Magic: An Introductory Treatise on the Basic Principles of Yellow Magic* by Isaac Bonewits. Though somewhat dated, this is the book that thousands of Wiccan teachers have used to train their students for thirty years.

*The Healing Craft: Healing Practices for Witches and Pagans* by Janet Farrar, Stuart Farrar, and Gavin Bone. The first Wiccan book I've seen specifically focused on the techniques and theories of healing body, mind, and spirit. An excellent resource.

*The Witch's Magical Handbook* and *Tantric Yoga: The Royal Path to Raising Kundalini Power* by Gavin Frost and Yvonne Frost. The first is a compendium of their unusual and fascinating approach to practical magic. For those who want to try actually doing Witchcraft as Gardner originally intended it to be done, the second book is another of the Frosts' clearheaded guides to an overly mystified topic.

*The Elements of Ritual* by Deborah Lipp. In depth discussion on the relationships between Wiccan ritual theory and practice and the classical concept of the four elements.

*The Pagan Book of Living and Dying: Practical Rituals, Prayers, Blessings, and Meditations on Crossing Over* by Starhawk and several others. Tools to help yourself or someone else die well.

*Advanced Wicca: Exploring Deeper Levels of Spiritual Skills and Masterful Magick* and *The Wiccan Book of Ceremonies and Rituals* by Patricia Telesco. These both go beyond the usual "Ritual 101" books and are well worth adding to any Wiccan library.

## Neopagan Witchcraft:
## Reference Books and Anthologies

*The Modern Craft Movement (Witchcraft Today, Book 1), Modern Rites of Passage (Book 2), Shamanism and Witchcraft (Book 3), and Living between Two Worlds: Challenges of the Modern Witch (Book 4)* by Chas Clifton (editor). This series of anthologies is excellent, containing essays by both Pagans and non-Pagans of widely varied scholarship.

*Witchcraft, Satanism and Occult Crime: Who's Who and What's What, a Manual of Reference Materials for the Professional Investigator* by the Church of All Worlds' Staff. An inexpensive yet invaluable tool for those concerned about "occult crime" and whether the neighborhood Pagans might be involved in "something terrible." Can be bought from the Church of All Worlds at www.caw.org. Give one to your local law enforcement agency.

*The Circle Guide to Pagan Groups* by Circle Sanctuary (see appendix 6). Lists Wiccan and other Neopagan groups primarily in the United States and Canada.

*The Law Enforcement Guide to Wicca* by Kerr Cuchulain. A manual written by a Canadian Neopagan police officer for his colleagues. This is the other title to give to your local police.

*Encyclopedia of Witches and Witchcraft,* 2nd edition, by Rosemary Ellen Guile. The latest revision to a solid work of general education (except that she seems a little too trusting of the tales some folks tell her about their origins).

*Being a Pagan: Druids, Wiccans and Witches Today* by Ellen Evert

Hopman and Lawrence Bond. This book of interviews is an excellent introduction to current thinking in the Neopagan community. Of course, I may be biased because Druids in general (and myself in particular) are interviewed first—a real change from the usual emphasis on Wicca. Wiccans are, however, inevitably the primary focus. Previously published as *People of the Earth: The New Pagans Speak Out.*

*Modern Pagans: An Investigation of Contemporary Pagan Practices* by V. Vale and John Sulak. This is another excellent book of interviews with British and American Neopagans, both famous and obscure. Look here to find dozens of pictures—including baby pictures!—of myself and other Neopagans.

## Historical Overviews

*History—Remembered, Recovered, Invented* by Bernard Lewis. A brief introduction to the ways in which people filter history through their personal and cultural needs, fears, and wishes, even when they're trying to be unbiased. Out of print, but well worth hunting for.

*The Witch in History: Early Modern and Twentieth-Century Representations* by Diane Purkiss. A feminist historian who doesn't allow her justified anger over historical atrocities against women to lead her into playing fast and loose with the facts, as she discusses all the different ways in which the image of the witch has been viewed in recent centuries.

*A History of Witchcraft: Sorcerers, Heretics, and Pagans* by Jeffrey B. Russell. An excellent overview, biased a bit by the author's career focus on dualist heresies and the history of the Christian Devil.

## An Important Series

The following titles are all good, solid academic scholarship. They are too expensive for most people to own, but you may be able to find them in a college or university library near you, or borrow them through an inter-library loan program:

*Witchcraft and Magic in Europe: Biblical and Pagan Societies* by Frederick H. Cryer, Marie-Louise Thomsen, Bengt Ankarloo, Stuart Clark.

*Witchcraft and Magic in Europe: Ancient Greece and Rome* by Bengt Ankarloo, Stuart Clark.

*Witchcraft and Magic in Europe: The Middle Ages* by Karen Jolly, Catharina Raudvere, Edward Peters, Bengt Ankarloo, Stuart Clark.

*Witchcraft and Magic in Europe: The Period of the Witch Trials* by Bengt Ankarloo, Stuart Clark, William Monter.

*Witchcraft and Magic in Europe: The Eighteenth and Nineteenth Centuries* by Bengt Ankarloo, Stuart Clark.

*Witchcraft and Magic in Europe: The Twentieth Century* by Bengt Ankarloo, Stuart Clark.

You will notice that there are very few books here from the Feminist Craft (other than Starhawk's and Patricia Monaghan's) or various supposed Hereditary Traditions of Witchcraft. That's because most of them have been of very poor quality over the years, as far as scholarship, logic, evidence of claims, or magical technique are concerned. However, some other good books have no doubt been overlooked, including some by friends and colleagues, so I will add them in future editions if people will politely bring them to my attention.

APPENDIX 6

# On and Offline Wiccan Resources

### Networking Sites

**The Witches' Voice** can be found on the Net at www.witchvox.com. It has the world's largest existing database of Wiccan and other Neopagan contacts, as well as a huge library of articles and essays about Neopagan Witchcraft and other Pagan paths, plus a section designed for the needs of professional journalists.

**America Online** has a very lively and active Neopagan community (many of whom are Wiccans), with chat rooms, libraries of text and graphics files, and message boards. Use the keyword "Pagan" to access these.

There are over 2,500 Wiccan and other Pagan e-lists/groups, running from half a dozen members to 1,000+, of wildly varying knowledge at **Yahoo Groups,** www.yahoogroups.com.

There are many Wiccan and other Pagan "groups" that can be found on **MSN Groups,** communities.msn.com. These are like the older "BBSs" of the 1980s and '90s.

### Group Sites

The **Aquarian Tabernacle Church** (ATC) has its Web site at www.aquatabch.org. This is one of the largest Wiccan churches in the world, with legal recognition in the United States and other countries. The ATC provides a legal "umbrella" for qualifying covens desiring legal and tax-exempt status. Its e-mail address is atc@aquatabch.org. It can be reached offline at Box 409, Index, WA 98258 USA.

The **Church and School of Wicca,** run by the Wiccan authors Gavin Frost and Yvonne Frost, has its Web site at www.wicca.org. The Frosts offer correspondence courses, books, videos, annual get-togethers, and so on related to Frostian Wicca. Their e-mail address is school@citynet.net. They can be written to via Box 297, Hinton, WV 25951 USA.

**Circle Sanctuary** can be found on the net at www.circlesanctuary. org. It is "a non-profit Nature Spirituality center serving Wiccan, Shamanic, Goddess, Druidic, Celtic Mystic, and other Pagan folk worldwide." It publishes the *Circle Guide to Pagan Groups* and *Circle Magazine*, both of which are major networking tools. Its e-mail address is circle@mhtc.net. It can be written to via Box 219, Mt. Horeb, WI, 53572 USA.

The **Covenant of the Goddess (COG)** at www.cog.org is "an international organization of cooperating, autonomous Wiccan congregations and solitary practitioners." It provides 501(c) (3) tax-exempt status as branch congregations to qualifying covens, as well as educational materials and advice to Wiccans dealing with the media. Its e-mail address is info@cog.org. Write to it via Box 1226, Berkeley, CA, 94701 USA.

**Spiral Scouts** (www.spiralscouts.org) are a nonsexist, nonhomophobic scouting program for Neopagan girls and boys, as well as members of other minority faiths and lifestyles.

I should also list my own Web site, www.neopagan.net. While not focused on Wicca, it does contain articles and information of general Neopagan, Druidic, and magical interest.

There are also many online and offline newsletters, magazines, and journals of Neopaganism and Witchcraft that can be found in your local esoteric, occult, or New Age store, as well as tracked down through the Web sites listed in this section.

These facts were good as of October 2005. These are mostly institutions that have been around for many years and are likely to remain so. If one of the Web site or e-mail addresses fails, search for current ones via major Web search sites.

# Reconciling with the Moon*

## BY ASHLEEN O'GAEA

*I asked Ashleen if I could include her review of Hutton's work, not only because I agree with almost everything she says but also because much of what she says about the need for Wiccans to accept and take pride in our true history applies to my research as well. [Words in square brackets are mine.]*

 onald Hutton, a Professor of History at the University of Bristol, has written a book called *The Triumph of the Moon: A History of Modern Pagan Witchcraft*. The book is well researched, clearly and cogently presented, encouraging, and respectful. It's important for all those (and other) reasons—*and* because it will be devastating to some of us.

The friend who recommended that I read this book told me, "It blows everything out of the water." I listened, stunned, as he explained that Hutton debunks all our myths; and when I started reading it, I reacted with the anger my friend had predicted. From etymology to events, Hutton deconstructs our history.

No, he says, Wicca wasn't handed down in secret through persecuted generations. This bit came from Masonic ritual, that from ceremonial magic, and the other from the Romantic poets or the Order of Woodcraft Chivalry. The genealogy he uncovers for modern Wicca is not disinteresting or dishonorable, just very dramatically different from the history most of us take for granted. But "Triumph of the Moon" is not a cynical or sarcastic title, and Hutton hasn't left us for

*First published in *Circle Magazine*, Summer 2001, © 2001 by Ashleen O'Gaea.

dead. The more I refer to it, the better I like it; I hope to convince you not only to read it, but to see it as more hope and glory than gloom and doom.

Hutton calls it to our attention in his Preface that this "claims to be *a* history and not *the* history." He describes his work as:

> the first systematic attempt by a professional historian to characterize and account for this aspect of modern Western culture. As such it is an exploratory and tentative work, intended as an initial mapping out of an area which badly needs and deserves serious treatment by more scholars. . . . In *Pagan Religions of the Ancient British Isles*, I took notice of the fact that Pagan religions existed in the modern British Isles, which sometimes claimed to represent an unbroken continuity of those who were my principle subject. Virtually all academic scholars of ancient Paganism until that time had either ignored them (or in the case of Druids) cursorily dismissed them. My own book came down heavily against the claim of continuity, and, indeed, the notion that modern Paganisms had very much in common with those of the ancient world. On the other hand, I also formed the opinion that they were perfectly viable modern religions in their own right.

He then began to wonder "where, when, and why they had in fact arisen, if they had not survived continuously." *The Triumph of the Moon* lays out the answers he's found to those questions.

In the backs of our minds at least, most of us have known three things for a while. One, our emotional dependence on Wicca's being an ancient religion reflects a patriarchal standard that is both inappropriate to our cosmology and beneath our dignity to accept. Two, Margaret Murray's and Sir James Frazer's scholarship proves to be inadequate by today's standards. Three, "Gardner made it all up."

Writers like Bonewits and Kelly have been telling us so for some time, but because Bonewits wasn't [known to be] Wiccan and Kelly was "out to discredit Gardner," it was relatively easy to table their work, or ignore it, or deny it. Many of us took various related professional and scholarly debates to be fueled as much by conservatism and sexism as anything else.

Hutton's different, though. He's got a decent academic reputation, he's an expert in relevant fields, and he had access to primary sources. Just as important, however, is that he has no axe to grind, no point to prove. Throughout *Triumph* he is respectful of Wicca and consistently treats it as the real and legitimate religion it is. There is even a subtle undercurrent, I think, of excitement about Wicca's documentable history. We can't refuse to take Hutton seriously, and we can't ignore his challenge to Wicca's traditional history.

We must at last, however regretfully, consciously acknowledge that our beloved Medieval Witchcraft—the peasants' generations of proto-Wicca that disappeared into secret, sacred woods and hills while the Inquisition raged across the land, barely surviving till Gardner gave it public life again—never existed. Contrary to the slogan that Bonewits coined, "Never again the Burning," the truth seems to be "Never even once the Burning." As Hutton says, "[It is] established beyond any reasonable doubt that there was no long-lasting or wide-ranging persecution of witches in early modern Europe" [although, it depends on your definitions of all the words in that sentence].

Gardner, of course, didn't know that—he and most of his contemporaries accepted Murray's and Frazer's interpretation. It was "common knowledge" in his day that ancient Pagan religions survived the Inquisition by going underground, that those Pagan religions had been matriarchal, worshiping a Great Mother and Her horned consort, and that folk-tales represented memories of those ancient rites and ways. When Gardner developed Wicca, he sincerely understood himself to be redeveloping and restoring it. Those elements he knew not to be literally true he felt were spiritually, symbolically, or poetically true. I think he was right.

"It should be said that there is nothing inherently implausible in Gardner's claim to have been initiated into an existing religion," Hutton admits. But how much of himself Gardner put into the history of the New Forest coven is, I think, not the most significant aspect of the new truth Hutton tells us. In fact, my estimation of

Gardner is rising as I see the magnitude of his accomplishment in Hutton's brighter light.

Once, the lack of evidence for ancestral Wicca's survival seemed reasonable: what evidence would a secret cult leave? But as Hutton says,

> [S]tudies of heterodoxy in the period [1400–1800] have revealed that it is possible to track even tiny and secretive sects through the centuries, both through their own private papers and literature and the observations of outsiders, whether neighbors or local or central authorities. This is true even of the sixteenth century, let alone the seventeenth, when the breakdown of central controls during the Civil War allowed sectarian groups to flourish.

Gardner didn't have to address this new scholarship; but we do [see my comments about the maranos in chapter 5].

By the early 1900s, Hutton's research suggests, British culture had been articulating a need for Pagan energy for about 100 years. Romantic poets from the mid-1800s on had been rhapsodizing about the English countryside as a last bastion of peace and quiet, and natural pleasures and transactions—a haven against the clogged and polluted urban centers which demoralized humanity. The "Merry England" movement was in full swing (and hasn't slacked off much since), and Christianity, along with attendant hierarchies and parallel authorities, was under attack from the arts and sciences.

In the process of laying all this out for us, Hutton does show that most of Wicca's history is, in fact, a myth. But story breaking isn't his intent, and Wiccan readers need to stop the habit of responding defensively to new information. Never mind that there's still a scholarly debate over the origin and meaning of several of "our words," including "witch"; as Dr. M. Scott Peck reminds us in *The Different Drum*, everything is overdetermined (has more than one cause or origin). One of the roots of witch means "bend or shape," and I see no reason to give that up when it's worked so well so far. Thus, I propose to do a little bending and shaping here—not of the facts as we now must admit them, but of our approach and interpretation of them. Here's the story I "hear" in Hutton's work:

In the time before time, the Great Mother and Her horned Consort were worshiped universally, in various rites around the world. When Christianity emerged, there was a short period of "peaceful" co-existence, then a period of struggle, and—here's the part I'm getting from Hutton—then Paganism was pretty effectively wiped out. We can guess there must've been *something* going on as late as the 12th–13th centuries, when laws against specific Pagan practices were still being written, but there's no evidence for survival after that.

Hutton's previous works, *The Pagan Religions of the Ancient British Isle, Stations of the Sun,* and *The Rise and Fall of Merry England* all showed that modern Paganism hasn't much in common with the ancient style, and we may tend to bristle about that, but we don't need to. Any organized Paganism, with its personal responsibility (authority as well as accountability), and parity for women, was gone by the time the Inquisition was declared. About 40–50,000 people were executed for "witchcraft," one of many heresies the Church opposed, and none of them were "us."

But . . . but . . .

I think what happened is that Christianity did take over, had hundreds of years to make its best case, and was eventually found lacking in several respects. There were some consequences of the Inquisition years to deal with. There was a huge redistribution of wealth following the plagues' decimations of the population. An economic middle class gradually developed, and so did the Reformation, and the Enlightenment. All these changes kept things stirred up for a few centuries. But once the dust settled, people began to realize that the extant theology left something to be desired. Specifically, it left a *Goddess* to be desired

This desire was ever more specifically and insistently articulated in the 150 or so years before Gardner's lifetime. Reading Hutton, it's clear that the arts and social sciences—proper voices to declare longings of the heart, don't you think?—had been preparing British culture for a restoration of a natural relationship to God(s). The Romantic poets' work was full of fair countrysides peopled by wise men and wise women who knew the ancient lore of healing, and villagers who kept the old ways still.

The Industrial Revolution's developing social and political institutions were as intrusive and overbearing as the Church, and drove more and more people to Pagan country idylls and havens, real or imagined. Freudian and Jungian psychology had an effect. The far-reaching effects of colonialism were factors. Leland's *Aradia*, which he and many others wholly believed was evidence for Murray's and Frazer's theories, had an effect. Pan and Diana were still there—one only had to seek them out or, maybe, draw them out from within.

Typically of his underlying attitude toward points of Wiccan theology, Hutton puts it this way as he closes his third chapter:

> . . . I am not necessarily suggesting that the deities themselves are in fact imaginary. Much of the tone of the past two chapters may be taken to imply that they are nothing more than projections— even if passionate projections—of the human heart and mind. This may well be so. It may equally well be true, however, that human belief has actually given them life, or else that they have always existed and have been perceived anew because people now have need of them. These are questions which no historian—indeed no human—can resolve, and the functional nature of my idiom should not be allowed to obscure that fact.

What this book has shown me is that Gardner didn't "make it up" so much as he restored something he believed to have survived by the skin of its teeth. He might even have been an Avatar [a human who incarnates a deity]. Hutton might agree. "In religious terms, it might be said that he was contacted by a divine force which had been manifesting with increasing strength during the previous two hundred years, and that it worked through him to remarkable effect," he says in his chapter about Gardner.

The now-we-know-it's-a myth that Murray and Frazer boosted and several cultural pillars supported is still a precious story, and has a lot of life left in it. If the life it has comes from our belief, and us, we have both the right and the responsibility to understand that lineage as successful magic, or even a miracle, and not a calamity.

Remember the movie *E.T.* and the scene where the space-suited scientists took over the house? That sequence was shot from a really low angle so that the scientists would look as scary to the audience as they did to young Henry. "Our" story about the Medieval Witches (Charlie Murphy's "The Burning Times" is still a Wiccan anthem) turns out to be told from the same low angle, and it expresses the same sort of psycho-emotional truth as that scene in *E.T.*—*It's not a lie, it's a perspective.* We don't have to stop telling this story, we just have to start hearing it differently.

At the same time, we can be proud of a new story: we really are "the Witches, back from the dead," as one of the lines asserts in "We Are the Flow, We Are the Ebb," a popular Pagan chant. What Paganism there was, was literally killed, and was so sorely grieved and missed that it had to be brought back. Hutton catalogues a growing longing for Her through the 18th–19th centuries, and makes it as plain as your cat's nudges for attention. If no one else but Gardner could have revived it, then we should be even more impressed with the synchronicity [and his genius].

Wicca's still growing, and not just because everybody likes the pointy hats so well. Wicca is growing because the theology and cosmology makes sense to people. If there were no Wiccan-style witches before (about) 1950, well, it's their loss! Fascinating details, interesting new connections, appreciation of a well-written book, and the value of knowledge for its own sake aside, Hutton's book, like Bonewits's, doesn't have to be devastating at all. It can, in fact, boost our energy considerably.

Both authors hope their work will inspire more research—and it should; there's no lack of threads to follow. Not having to maintain an allegiance to the literal truth of the medieval underground Witchcraft story frees us to uncover more of our real history, and to understand our mythic history in new ways.

And, listen to this! In another few hundred years, say by the next millennium, *our Wicca will be ancient.* That means that what we're doing today is establishing Wicca's ancient traditions. None of us, not once we've read Hutton, anyway, can think we are just "following" this religion. We are all reviving and creating this religion, still making its history. We are our own "ancestors in faith."

It's really even more exciting when you think of this line from the *Charge of the Goddess:* ". . . for if that which you seek you do not find within yourself, you shall surely never find it without." Well, we've now found that it *was* within ourselves before we found it without (and that's true about the way many of us came to Wicca, too). We find it without because we create it from within. Could it be more fitting that this is how Wicca emerged?

Hutton considers Wicca's legitimacy as a full-fledged religion, too, and his discussion of Wicca in a beautifully named chapter, "Grandchildren of the Shadows," is a pleasure to read. It's good to see how close American and British Wicca really are, when the differences tend to get the emphasis; and we all need reminding now and again of the enormous progress we've made since 1950. He reviews the categories of religion presently recognized—cult, sect, new religious movement, native religion, nature religion, post-modern religion—and Wicca, he thinks, fits easily into none of these categories.

> A new classification might be proposed here, of "revived religion." This is the only one . . . which truly does justice to what is arguably the central and enduring characteristic of Pagan Witchcraft; that it is a modern development which deliberately draws upon ancient images and ideas for contemporary needs, as part of a wholesale rejection of the faiths which have been dominant since the ancient ways of worship were suppressed.
>
> The true conceptual significance of Paganism, including Pagan Witchcraft [he concludes], is that it occupies the ground at which nature religion, post-modern religion, and revived religion intersect. None of these is a religious model which scholars trained in traditional history, theology, sociology, and anthropology find easy to understand; which is probably why, although Pagan Witchcraft has had a prominent public profile in Britain for half a century, it has been much less studied than other religious movements

which have appeared or arrived more recently. Perhaps the present
book will do something to alter that pattern.

Let's be true to our history, live our myth, and take a hand in the
alterations. Read Hutton's book, and let it change the pattern of your
thought about Wicca and its history. Let *Triumph's* microhistories in-
trigue and delight you; let Hutton's references fill your reading list for
summers to come! Go beyond the standard hagiographies and get to
know the founders of our faith as the very human men and women
they were—and let yourself be awed as you try to imagine doing the
work they did! We may deeply mourn the crossing of our underground ancestors to the realms of myth, yet through this loss we can
still rely on Her promise of "peace, freedom, and reunion with
those who have gone before." This contingency has been provided
for: ". . . to be reborn, you must die, and to die you must be born,
and without love you may not be born; and this is all the magic."
    Hutton's not rewriting our theology, and our beliefs do not depend
on the literal truth of our myths. Be at peace in the knowledge that
though Pagan sites and rites may have been overcome, the Goddess
did not die, nor did people's need for Goddess. On the contrary, people's love for Her was so great that it brought Her Witches (that's us!)
back from the dead. Goddess is alive and magic is afoot—embrace
this new freedom to explore other aspects of Wiccan myth and liturgy. (Our mythical ancestors are free now too, from our narrow imag-
inings, to join us in more thorough explorations of the inner realms.)
And we can merrier meet our historical forebears again, with a renewed and extended appreciation of their achievements.
    One of Starhawk's best-known contributions to Wiccan liturgy is
the chant, "She changes everything She touches, and everything She
touches changes." Bearing in mind the obvious implication of Starhawk's chant that if you're not changing, She's not touching you, read
Hutton's book and adjust yourself to the new reality. Read what the
Goddess has written in your aura and on your soul, and be reconciled
with the Moon.

# Recent Developments in the Study of the Great European Witch Hunt

## BY JENNY GIBBONS

ince the late 1970s, a quiet revolution has taken place in the study of historical witchcraft and the Great European Witch Hunt. The revolution wasn't quite as dramatic as the development of radio-carbon dating, but many theories which reigned supreme thirty years ago have vanished, swept away by a flood of new data. Unfortunately, little of the new information has made it into popular history. Many articles in Pagan magazines contain almost no accurate information about the "Burning Times," primarily because we rely so heavily on out-dated research.

## Beyond the National Enquirer

What was this revolution? Starting in the mid-1970s, historians stopped relying on witch-hunting propaganda and began to base their theories on thorough, systematic studies of all the witch trials in a particular area. Ever since the Great Hunt itself, we've relied on witch hunters' propaganda: witch hunting manuals, sermons against witchcraft, and lurid pamphlets on the more sensational trials. Everyone knew that this evidence was lousy. It's sort of like trying to study Satanism in America using only the *Moral Majority Newsletter* and the *National Enquirer.* The few trials cited were the larger, more infamous ones. And historians frequently used literary accounts of those cases, not the trials themselves. That's comparable to citing a television docu-drama ("Based on a true story!") instead of actual court proceedings.

Better evidence did exist. Courts that tried witches kept records— trial verdicts, lists of confiscated goods, questions asked during inter-rogations, and the answers witches gave. This evidence was written by people who knew what actually happened. Witch hunters often based their books on rumor and hearsay; few had access to reliable informa-tion. Courts had less reason to lie since, for the most part, they were trying to keep track of what was going on: how many witches they killed, how much money they gained or lost, etc. Witch hunters wrote to convince people that witchcraft was a grievous threat to the world. The more witches there were, the bigger the "threat" was. So they often exaggerated the number of deaths and spread wild esti-mates about how many witches existed. Also, trial records addressed the full range of trials, not just the most lurid and sensational ones.

But trial data had one daunting draw-back: there was too much of it. Witch trials were scattered amongst literally millions of other trials from this period. For most historians, it was too much work to wade through this mass of data. The one exception was C. L'Estrange Ewen. In 1929 he published the first systematic study of a country's trial records: *Witch Hunting and Witch Trials.* Focused on England, his work offered vivid evidence of how much data literature missed. In Essex County, for instance, Ewen found thirty times as many trials as any previous researcher. Scholars were basing their theories on only 3 percent of the available evidence. And that 3 percent was vastly dif-ferent from the other 97 percent.

In the 1970s other researchers followed in Ewen's footsteps, so in the last twenty-five years, the quantity and quality of available evi-dence has dramatically improved. Now we can look at all the trials from an area and see what the "normal" trial was really like. Court documents frequently contain detailed information on the gender, social status, and occupation of the accused. Today, for the first time, we have a good idea of the dimensions of the Great Hunt: where the trials occurred, who was tried in them, who did the killing, and how many people lost their lives.

## 400 in One Day: An Influential Forgery

Another, smaller breakthrough also profoundly altered our view of the early history of the Great Hunt. In 1972, two scholars independently discovered that a famous series of medieval witch trials never happened.

The forgery was Etienne Leon de Lamothe-Langon's *Histoire de l'Inquisition en France,* written in 1829. Lamothe-Langon described enormous witch trials which supposedly took place in southern France in the early 14th century. Run by the Inquisition of Toulouse and Carcasonne, these trials killed hundreds upon hundreds of people. The most famous was a craze where 400 women died in one day. No other French historian had noticed these trials.

In the early 20th century, the prominent historian Jacob Hansen included large sections of Lamothe-Langon's work in his compendium on medieval witchcraft. Later historians cited Hansen's cites, apparently without closely examining Lamothe-Langon's credentials. Non-academic writers cited the writers who cited Hansen, and thus Lamothe-Langon's dramatic French trials became a standard part of the popular view of the Great Hunt.

However, as more research was done, Lamothe-Langon's trials began to look odd to historians. No sources mentioned them, and they were completely different from all other 14th century trials. There were no other mass trials of this nature until 1428, no panics like this until the 16th century. Furthermore, the demonology in the trials was quite elaborate, with sabbats and pacts and enormous black masses. It was far more complex than the demonology of the *Malleus*

*Maleficarum* (1486). Why would the Inquisition think up this elaborate demonology, and then apparently forget it for two hundred years?

Questions like these led Norman Cohn (*Europe's Inner Demons* and "Three Forgeries: Myths and Hoaxes of European Demonology II" in *Encounter 44* (1975)) and Richard Kieckhefer (*European Witch Trials*) to investigate Lamothe-Langon's background. What they found was reasonably conclusive evidence that the great trials of the *Histoire* had never occurred.

First, Lamothe-Langon was a hack writer and known forger, not a historian. Early in his career he specialized in historical fiction, but he soon turned to more profitable horror novels, like *The Head of Death, The Monastery of the Black Friars,* and *The Vampire* (or, *The Virgin of Hungary*). Then, in 1829, he published the *Histoire,* supposedly a work of non-fiction. After its success Lamothe-Langon went on to write a series of "autobiographies" of various French notables, such as Cardinal Richelieu, Louis XVIII, and the Comtesse du Barry.

Second, none of Lamothe-Langon's sources could be found, and there was strong reason to suspect they never existed. Lamothe-Langon claimed he was using unpublished Inquisitorial records given to him by Bishop Hyacinthe Sermet—Cohn found a letter from Sermet stating that there were no unpublished records. Lamothe-Langon had no training in paleography, the skill needed to translate the script and copious abbreviations used in medieval documents, and he was not posted in Toulouse long enough to do any serious research in its archives.

Third, under close examination a number of flaws appeared in his stories. He cited records written by seneschal Pierre de Voisins in 1275, but Voisins ceased being seneschal in 1254 and died not long after. The inquisitor who ran many of these trials was Pierre Guidonis (nephew of Bernard Gui from *The Name of the Rose*). But Guidonis wasn't an inquisitor at the time when the trials were held. Cohn and Kieckhefer published their findings in 1972. Since then academics have avoided this forged material. Unfortunately by this point, Lamothe-Langon's lurid trials had entered into the mythology of witchcraft.

While nobody cites Lamothe-Langon directly anymore, his fictions show up everywhere, including both Z Budapest's *The Holy Book of Women's Mysteries* and Raven Grimassi's *The Wiccan Mysteries*.

There's no simple way to weed out all of Lamothe-Langon's disinformation, but a few guidelines will help:

a. Use scholarly texts written after 1975.
b. Beware of any trial set in Toulouse or Carcasonne. While these cities did have real cases, only the forged ones get cited regularly.
c. Ignore any trial involving Anne-Marie de Georgel or Catherine Delort; they're forgeries.
d. Ignore any trial that killed "400 women in one day." This never happened.
e. Avoid Jules Michelet's *Satanism and Witchcraft*. Although he wrote a poetic and dramatic book, Michelet never found much historical evidence to support his theory that witchcraft was an anti-Catholic protest religion. What little bit there was came from the Lamothe-Langon forgeries. So when they were debunked, the last props for his book collapsed.
f. The appendix of Richard Kieckhefer's *European Witch Trials* contains a list of all known trials that occurred between 1300 and 1500.

## The New Geography of Witch Hunting

The pattern revealed by trial records bears little resemblance to the picture literature painted. Every aspect of the Great Hunt, from chronology to death toll, has changed. And if your knowledge of the "Burning Times" is based on popular or Pagan literature, nearly everything you know may be wrong.

**Chronology.** Popular history places the witchcraft persecutions in the Middle Ages (5th–14th centuries). 19th century historians considered the Great Hunt an outburst of superstitious hysteria, fostered and spread by the Catholic Church. "Naturally," therefore, the persecution would be worst when the Church's power was the greatest: in the Middle Ages, before the Reformation split "the" Church into warring Catholic and Protestant sects. Certainly there were trials in the early modern period (15th–18th centuries), but they must have been a pale shadow of the horrors that came before.

Modern research has debunked this theory quite conclusively. Although many stereotypes about witches pre-date Christianity, the lethal crazes of the Great Hunt were actually the child of the "Age of Reason." Lamothe-Langon's forged trials were one of the last stumbling blocks that kept the theory of medieval witch hunting alive, and once these trials are removed, the development of witchcraft stereotypes becomes much clearer. All pre-modern European societies believed in magick. As far as we can tell, all passed laws prohibiting magickal crimes. Pagan Roman law and the earliest Germanic and Celtic law codes all contain edicts that punish people who cast baneful spells. This is only common sense: a society that believes in the power of magick will punish people who abuse that power.

Many of the stereotypes about witches have been with us from pre-Christian times. From the Mediterranean to Ireland, witches were said to fly about at night, drinking blood, killing babies, and devouring human corpses. We know this because many early Christian missionaries encouraged newly converted kingdoms to pass laws protecting men and women from charges of witchcraft—charges, they said, that were impossible and un-Christian. For example, the 5th century Synod of St. Patrick ruled that "A Christian who believes that there is a vampire in the world, that is to say, a witch, is to be anathematized; whoever lays that reputation upon a living being shall not be received into the Church until he revokes with his own voice the crime that he has committed." A capitulary from Saxony (775–790 CE) blamed these stereotypes on Pagan belief systems: "If anyone, deceived by the Devil, believes after the manner of the pagans that any man or woman is a witch and eats men, and if on this ac-

count he burns [the alleged witch] . . . he shall be punished by capital sentence."

In the Middle Ages, the laws on magick remained virtually un-
changed. Harmful magick was punished, and the lethal trials we
know of tended to occur when a noble felt that he or she had been bewitched. The Church also forbade magick and assigned relatively
mild penalties to convicted witches. For instance, the Confessional of
Egbert (England, 950–1000 CE) said that "If a woman works witchcraft and enchantment and [uses] magical philters, she shall fast [on
bread and water] for twelve months. . . . If she kills anyone by her
philters, she shall fast for seven years."

Traditional attitudes towards witchcraft began to change in the
14th century, at the very end of the Middle Ages. As Carlo Ginzburg
noted (*Ecstasies: Deciphering the Witches' Sabbat*), early 14th century
central Europe was seized by a series of rumor-panics. Some malign
conspiracy (Jews and lepers, Moslems, or Jews and witches) was attempting to destroy the Christian kingdoms through magick and
poison. After the terrible devastation caused by the Black Death
(1347–49) these rumors increased in intensity and focused primarily
on witches and "plague-spreaders."

Witchcraft cases increased slowly but steadily from the 14th–15th
century. The first mass trials appeared in the 15th century. At the beginning of the 16th century, as the first shock-waves from the Reformation hit, the number of witch trials actually dropped. Then, around
1550, the persecution skyrocketed. What we think of as "the Burning
Times"—the crazes, panics, and mass hysteria—largely occurred in
one century, from 1550–1650. In the 17th century, the Great Hunt
passed nearly as suddenly as it had arisen. Trials dropped sharply after
1650 and disappeared completely by the end of the 18th century.

**Geography.** Before Lamothe-Langon's forgeries were discovered, the
earliest great hunts appeared to come from southern France, in an
area once the home of the Cathar heresy. This led some historians to
suggest a link between Catharism and witchcraft, that witches were

the remnants of an old dualist faith. After you delete the forged trials, the center of the early cases shifts to "Switzerland" and northern Italy, away from Cathar lands.

When all trials are plotted on a map, other surprising patterns emerge. First, the trials were intensely sporadic. The rate of witch hunting varied dramatically throughout Europe, ranging from a high of 26,000 deaths in Germany to a low of 4 in Ireland. Robin Briggs' *Witches and Neighbors* can give you a good feel for how erratic the trials were. It contains three maps showing the distribution of trials throughout Europe, throughout Germany, and throughout the French province of Lorraine, which Briggs studied in depth. They reveal that some of the most enormous persecutions (like the panics of Wurzburg, Germany) occurred next to areas that had virtually no trials whatsoever.

Second, the trials were concentrated in central Europe, in Germany, Switzerland, and eastern France. The further you got away from that area, the lower the persecution generally got.

Third, the height of the persecution occurred during the Reformation, when the formerly unified Christian Church shattered into Catholic and Protestant sects. In countries like Italy and Spain, where the Catholic Church and its Inquisition reigned virtually unquestioned, witch hunting was uncommon. The worst panics took place in areas like Switzerland and Germany, where rival Christians sects fought to impose their religious views on each other.

Fourth, panics clustered around borders. France's major crazes occurred on its Spanish and eastern fronts. Italy's worst persecution was in the northern regions. Spain's one craze centered on the Basque lands straddling the French/Spanish border.

Fifth, although it has become commonplace to think of the outbreaks of witch hunting as malevolent pogroms imposed by evil elites, in reality the worst horrors occurred where central authority had broken down. Germany and Switzerland were patchwork quilts, loose confederacies stitched together from dozens of independent political units. England, which had a strong government, had little witch hunting. The country's one and only craze took place during the English Civil War, when the government's power collapsed. A strong, unified national church (as in Spain and Italy) also tended to keep deaths to a minimum. Strong governments didn't always slow witch hunting, as King James of Scotland proved. But the worst panics definitely hit where both Church and State were weak.

**Christianity's Role in the Persecution.** For years, the responsibility for the Great Hunt has been dumped on the Catholic Church's doorstep. 19th century historians ascribed the persecution to religious hysteria. And when Margaret Murray proposed that witches were members of a Pagan sect, popular writers trumpeted that the Great Hunt was not a mere panic, but rather a deliberate attempt to exterminate Christianity's rival religion.

Today, we know that there is absolutely no evidence to support this theory. When the Church was at the height of its power (11th–14th centuries) very few witches died. Persecutions did not reach epidemic levels until after the Reformation, when the Catholic Church had lost its position as Europe's indisputable moral authority. Moreover most of the killing was done by secular courts. Church courts tried many witches but they usually imposed non-lethal penalties. A witch might be excommunicated, given penance, or imprisoned, but she was rarely killed. The Inquisition almost invariably pardoned any witch who confessed and repented.

Consider the case in York, England, as described by Keith Thomas (*Religion and the Decline of Magic*). At the height of the Great Hunt (1567–1640) one half of all witchcraft cases brought before church courts were dismissed for lack of evidence. No torture was used, and the accused could clear himself by providing four to eight "compurgators," people who were willing to swear that he wasn't a witch. Only 21 percent of the cases ended with convictions, and the Church did not impose any kind of corporal or capital punishment.

The vast majority of witches were condemned by secular courts. Ironically, the worst courts were local courts. Some authors, like Anne

Llewellyn Barstow (*Witchcraze*), blame the death toll on the decline of the "community-based" medieval court, and the rise of the centralized "national" court. Nothing could be further from the truth. "Community-based" courts were often virtual slaughterhouses, killing 90 percent of all accused witches. National courts condemned only about 30 percent of the accused.

Why were the execution rates so vastly different? Civil courts tended to handle "black" witchcraft cases, trials involving charges of magickal murder, arson, and other violent crimes. Church courts tried more "white" witchcraft: cases of magickal healing, divination, and protective magick. Trial evidence shows that courts always treated healing more leniently than cursing. Additionally, secular and religious courts served two different purposes. Civil courts "protected" society by punishing and killing convicted criminals. In theory, the Church's court system was designed to "save" the criminal—to make him or her a good Christian once more. Only unrepentant sinners were to be executed. The differences between local and national courts are also easy to explain. Witchcraft cases were usually surrounded by general fear and public protests. "Community-based" courts drew their officials from the community, the group of people affected by this panic. National courts had more distance from the hysteria. Moreover national courts tended to have professional, trained staff—men who were less likely to discard important legal safeguards in their haste to see "justice" done.

**The Inquisition.** But what of the Inquisition? For many, the "Inquisition" and the "Burning Times" are virtually synonymous. The myth of the witch-hunting inquisition was built on several assumptions and mistakes, all of which have been overturned in the last twenty-five years. First, the myth was the logical extension of 19th century history, which blamed the persecutions on the Catholic Church. If the Church attacked witches, surely the Inquisition would be the hammer She wielded.

Second, a common translation error muddied the waters. Many

records simply said that a witch was tried "by inquisition." Some writers assumed that this meant "the" Inquisition. And in some cases it did. But an "inquisition" was also the name of a type of trial used by almost all courts in Europe at the time. Later, when historians examined the records in greater detail, they found that the majority did not involve the Inquisition, merely an inquisition. Today most historians are careful about this, but older and more popular texts (such as Rossell Hope Robbins' *Encyclopedia of Witchcraft and Demonology*) still have the Inquisition killing witches in times and places where it did not even exist.

Third, the only witch-hunting manual most people have seen was written by an inquisitor. In the 1970s, when feminist and Neo-Pagan authors turned their attention to the witch trials, the *Malleus Maleficarum* (*Hammer of Witches*) was the only manual readily available in translation. Authors naively assumed that the book painted an accurate picture of how the Inquisition tried witches. Heinrich Kramer, the text's demented author, was held up as a typical inquisitor. His rather stunning sexual preoccupations were presented as the Church's "official" position on witchcraft. Actually the Inquisition immediately rejected the legal procedures Kramer recommended and censured the inquisitor himself just a few years after the *Malleus* was published. Secular courts, not inquisitorial ones, resorted to the *Malleus*. [But it went through dozens of editions in several languages, so it was not unimportant.—IB]

As more research was done and historians became more sensitive to the "an inquisition/the Inquisition" error, the inquisitorial witch-hunter began to look like a rare bird. Lamothe-Langon's trials were the last great piece of "evidence," and when they fell, scholars reexamined the Inquisition's role in the Burning Times. What they found was quite startling. In 1258 Pope Alexander IV explicitly refused to allow the Inquisition from investigating charges of witchcraft: "The Inquisitors, deputed to investigate heresy, must not intrude into investigations of divination or sorcery without knowledge of manifest heresy involved." The gloss on this passage explained what "manifest heresy" meant: "praying at the altars of idols, to offer sacrifices, to consult demons, to elicit responses from them . . . or if [the witches] associate themselves publicly with heretics." In other words, in the 13th century the Church did not consider witches heretics or members of a rival religion.

It wasn't until 1326, almost 100 years later, that the Church reversed its position and allowed the Inquisition to investigate witchcraft. But the only significant contribution that was made was in the development of "demonology," the theory of the diabolic origin of witchcraft. As John Tedeschi demonstrates in his essay "Inquisitorial Law and the Witch" (in Bengt Ankarloo and Gustav Henningsen's *Early Modern European Witchcraft*) the Inquisition still played a very small role in the persecution. From 1326–1500, few deaths occurred. Richard Kieckhefer (*European Witch Trials*) found 702 definite executions in all of Europe from 1300–1500; of these, only 137 came from inquisitorial or church courts. By the time that trials were common (early 16th century) the Inquisition focused on the proto-Protestants. When the trials peaked in the 16th and 17th century, the Inquisition was only operating in two countries: Spain and Italy, and both had extremely low death tolls.

In fact, in Spain the Inquisition worked diligently to keep witch trials to a minimum. Around 1609, a French witch-craze triggered a panic in the Basque regions of Spain. Gustav Henningsen (*The Witches' Advocate*) documented the Inquisition's work in brilliant detail. Although several inquisitors believed the charges, one skeptic convinced La Suprema (the ruling body of the Spanish Inquisition) that this was groundless hysteria. La Suprema responded by issuing an "Edict of Silence" forbidding all discussion of witchcraft. For, as the skeptical inquisitor noted, "There were neither witches nor bewitched until they were talked and written about."

The Edict worked, quickly dissipating the panic and accusations. And until the end of the Great Hunt, the Spanish Inquisition insisted that it alone had the right to condemn witches—which it refused to do. Another craze broke out in Vizcaya, in 1616. When the

Inquisition re-issued the Edict of Silence, the secular authorities went over their head and petitioned the king for the right to try witches themselves. The king granted the request, and 289 people were quickly sentenced. Fortunately the Inquisition managed to re-assert its monopoly on trials and dismissed all the charges. The "witches" of Cataluña were not so lucky. Secular authorities managed to execute 300 people before the Inquisition could stop the trials.

**The Witches.** Court records showed that there was no such thing as an "average" witch: there was no characteristic that the majority of witches shared, in all times and places. Not gender. Not wealth. Not religion. Nothing. The only thing that united them was the fact that they were accused of witchcraft. The diversity of witches is one of the strongest arguments against the theory that the Great Hunt was a deliberate pogrom aimed at a specific group of people. If that was true, then most witches would have something in common.

We can isolate certain factors that increased a person's odds of being accused. Most witches were women [though there were regions where most were men, as in Iceland—IB]. Many were poor or elderly; many seem to be unmarried. Most were alienated from their neighbors, or seen as "different" and disliked. But there is no evidence that one group was targeted. Traditional magick users might have a slightly higher chance of being accused of witchcraft, but the vast majority of known "white" witches were never charged.

Before trial evidence was available, there were two major theories on who the witches were. Margaret Murray (*The Witch Cult in Western Europe* and *The God of the Witches*) proposed that witches were members of a Pagan sect that worshipped the Horned God. Murray's research was exceptionally poor, and occasionally skated into outright textual manipulation. She restricted her studies to our worst evidence: witch hunting propaganda and trials that involved copious amounts of torture. She then assumed that such evidence was basically accurate, and that the Devil was "really" a Pagan god. None of these assumptions have held up under scrutiny.

In 1973, Barbara Ehrenreich and Deirdre English suggested that most witches were midwives and female healers. Their book *Witches, Midwives, and Nurses* convinced many feminists and Pagans that the Great Hunt was a pogrom aimed at traditional women healers. The Church and State sought to break the power of these women by accusing them of witchcraft, driving a wedge of fear between the wise-woman and her clients.

The evidence for this theory was—and is—completely anecdotal. The authors cited a number of cases involving healers, then simply assumed that this was what the "average" trial was like. However a mere decade after *Witches, Midwives, and Nurses* was published, we knew that this was not true. Healers made up a small percentage of the accused, usually between 2 percent and 20 percent, depending on the country. There was never a time or a place where the majority of accused witches were healers. In 1990, D. Harley's article, "Historians as Demonologists: The Myth of the Midwife-Witch" (in *Social History of Medicine 3* (1990), pp. 1–26) demonstrated that being a licensed midwife actually decreased a woman's chances of being charged.

And there was worse to come. Feminist and Pagan writers presented the healer-witch as the innocent, enlightened victim of the evil male witch hunters. Trials showed that as often as not, the "white" witch was an avid supporter of the "Burning Times." Diane Purkiss (*The Witch in History*) pointed out that "midwives were more likely to be found helping witch-hunters" than as victims of their inquiries. How did witches become witch-hunters? By blaming illnesses on their rivals. Feminist authors rightly lambasted male doctors who blamed unexplained illnesses on witches. Trial records suggest that this did happen, though not terribly often. If you look at doctors' case books you find that in most cases doctors found natural causes when people thought they were bewitched. When they did diagnose witchcraft, doctors almost never blamed a particular healer or witch. They were trying to explain their failure, not to destroy some individual.

Traditional healers and "white" witches routinely blamed diseases on witchcraft. For a doctor, diagnosing "witchcraft" was admitting failure. Medicine could do nothing against magick, and doctors were loathe to admit that they were powerless against a disease. However baneful magick was the forte of the helpful (or "white" witch). Folk healers regularly blamed illnesses on magick and offered counter-spells to cure their patients. Many were even willing to divine the name of the cursing witch, for a fee.

**Gender Issues.** One basic fact about the Great Witch Hunt stands out: most of the people accused were women. Even during the Hunt itself, commentators noticed this. Some speculated that there were 10,000 female witches for every male witch, and a host of misogynist explanations were trotted out to account for this fact. Later, the pre-dominance of women led some feminists to theorize that "witch" and "woman" were virtually synonymous, that the persecution was caused by Europe's misogyny.

Overall, approximately 75–80 percent of the accused were women. However this percentage varied dramatically. In several of the Scandi-navian countries, equal numbers of men and women were accused. In Iceland over 90 percent of the accused were men. Central Europe killed the most witches, and it killed many more women than men—this is why the overall percentages are so badly skewed.

Proponents of the misogyny theory generally ignore these varia-tions. Many simply do not discuss male witches. One of the most egregious examples comes from Anne Llewellyn Barstow's *Witch-craze*. Barstow says that Iceland did not have a "real" witch hunt. Now, Iceland killed more witches than Ireland, Russia, and Portugal combined. Barstow claims that all these countries had "real" hunts, and offers no explanation of what made Iceland's deaths "unreal." The only thing I can see is that almost all Icelandic witches were men, and Barstow's theory cannot handle that. [Gibbons may be missing the witch hunt/witchcraze distinction Barstow makes.—IB]

Given the sexism of the times, it's not difficult to find shockingly misogynist witch trials. But misogyny does not explain the trial pat-terns we see. The beginning and end of the persecution don't correlate to any notable shifts in women's rights. Trials clustered around borders—are borders more misogynist than interior regions? Ireland killed four witches, Scotland a couple thousand—are the Scots that much more sexist? Barstow admits that Russia was every bit as misogynist as Germany, yet it killed only ten witches. Her theory can't explain why, and so she simply insists that there were probably lots of other Russian witches killed and they were probably mostly women. We've just lost all the evidence that would support her theory.

## From Nine Million to Forty Thousand

The most dramatic changes in our vision of the Great Hunt centered on the death toll. Back before trial surveys were available, estimates of the death toll were almost 100 percent pure speculation. The only thing our literary evidence told us was that a lot of witches died. Witch hunting propaganda talked about thousands and thousands of executions. Literature focused on crazes, the largest and most sensational trials around. But we had no idea how accurate the literary evidence was, or how common trials actually were. So early death toll estimates, which ranged from several hundred thousand up to a high of nine million, were simply people trying to guess how much "a lot" of witches was.

Today, the process is completely different. Historians begin by counting all the executions/trials listed in an area's court records. Next they estimate how much evidence we've lost: what years and courts we're missing data for. Finally they survey the literary evidence, to see if any large witch trials occurred during the gaps in the evidence. There's still guess-work involved in today's estimates and many areas have not yet been systematically studied. But we now have a solid data-base to build our estimates from, and our figures are getting more specific as further areas are studied.

When the first trial record studies were completed, it was obvious that early estimates were fantastically high. Trial evidence showed that witch crazes were not everyday occurrences, as literature suggested. In fact most countries only had one or two in all of the Great Hunt. To date, less than 15,000 definite executions have been discovered in all of Europe and America combined. Even though many records are missing, it is now clear that death tolls higher than 100,000 are not believable.

Three scholars have attempted to calculate the total death toll for the Great Hunt using the new evidence. Brian Levack (*The Witch Hunt in Early Modern Europe*) surveyed regional studies and found that there were approximately 110,000 witch trials. Levack focused on recorded trials, not executions, because in many cases we have evidence that a trial occurred but no indication of its outcome. On average, 48 percent of trials ended in an execution, therefore he estimated that 60,000 witches died. This is slightly higher than 48 percent to reflect the fact that Germany, the center of the persecution, killed more than 48 percent of its witches.

Ronald Hutton (*The Pagan Religions of the British Isles* and "Counting the Witch Hunt," an unpublished essay) used a different methodology. First he surveyed the regional studies and counted up the number of estimated deaths they contained. When he ran into an uncounted area, he looked for a counted area which matched it as closely as possible, in terms of population, culture, and the intensity of witch hunting mentioned in literary evidence. He then assumed that the uncounted area would kill roughly as many witches as the counted area. Using this technique, he estimated that 40,000 witches died in the Great Hunt.

Anne Llewellyn Barstow (*Witchcraze*) estimated that 100,000 witches died, but her reasoning was flawed. Barstow began with Levack's 60,000 deaths. Then she increased it to 100,000 for two reasons: 1) To compensate for lost records; and 2) Because new trials are still being found.

This may sound reasonable, but it's not. The 110,000 estimated witch trials that Levack based his calculations on already did contain a large allowance for lost records. Barstow was apparently unaware of this, and added more deaths for no good reason. Her point about new trials is true, but irrelevant. Yes, more deaths are being discovered each year. But the more we find, the lower the death toll goes. This makes sense once you understand how historians make their estimates. "New" trials aren't trials we never dreamed existed. They appear when we count areas and courts that haven't been counted before. Historians have always known that our data was imperfect, and they always included estimates for lost trials. So when you find "new" executions, you can't simply add them to the total death toll: you also have to subtract the old estimate they're replacing. And since old estimates were generally far too high, newly "found" trials usually end up lowering the death toll.

## Why It Matters

These changes make it critically important to use up-to-date research if you're investigating historical witchcraft. We have perhaps 20 times as much information as we had two decades ago. Witchcraft studies has also become an inter-disciplinary field. Once the domain of historians alone, it now attracts anthropologists and sociologists who offer radically new interpretations of the Great Hunt. Anthropologists point out the ubiquity of witchcraft beliefs, demonstrating that the Great Hunt was not an exclusively European phenomenon. Sociologists draw chilling parallels between the Great Hunt and recent panics over Satanic cults, evidence which hints that we're still not out of the shadow of the Burning Times.

We Neopagans now face a crisis. As new data appeared, historians altered their theories to account for it. We have not. Therefore an enormous gap has opened between the academic and the "average" Pagan view of witchcraft. We continue to use out-dated and poor writers, like Margaret Murray, Montague Summers, Gerald Gardner, and Jules Michelet. We avoid the somewhat dull academic texts that present solid research, preferring sensational writers who play to our emotions. For example, I have never seen a copy of Brian Levack's *The Witch Hunt in Early Modern Europe* in a Pagan bookstore. Yet half the stores I visit carry Anne Llewellyn Barstow's *Witchcraze,* a deeply flawed book which has been ignored or reviled by most scholarly historians.

We owe it to ourselves to study the Great Hunt more honestly, in more detail, and using the best data available. Dualistic fairy tales of noble witches and evil witch hunters have great emotional appeal, but they blind us to what happened. And what could happen, today. Few Pagans commented on the haunting similarities between the Great Hunt and America's panic over Satanic cults. Scholars noticed it; we didn't. We say "Never again the Burning!" But if we don't know what happened the first time, how are we ever going to prevent it from happening again?

JENNY GIBBONS has an M.A. in medieval history and minored in the history of the Great Hunt. You can contact her at jennyg@compuserve. com. This article originally appeared in issue #5 of *Pomegranate* (Lammas, 1998).

# About the Author

Isaac Bonewits is North America's leading expert on ancient and modern Druidism, Witchcraft, and the rapidly growing Earth Religions movement. A practicing Neopagan priest, scholar, teacher, bard, and polytheologian for over thirty years, he has coined much of the vocabulary and articulated many of the issues that have shaped the rapidly growing Neopagan community, with opinions both playful and controversial.

As an author, a singer-songwriter, and a "spellbinding" speaker, he has educated, enlightened, and entertained two generations of modern Goddess worshippers, nature mystics, and followers of other minority belief systems and has explained these movements to journalists, law enforcement officers, college students, and academic researchers.

As of early 2006, he lives with his wife, Phaedra, his son Arthur, and too many critters in Rockland County, New York, a reasonably safe twenty-five miles away from Manhattan.